WOOD

for woodturners

WOOD
for woodturners

Mark Baker

with a foreword by Bert Marsh

GUILD OF MASTER CRAFTSMAN
PUBLICATIONS LTD

First published 2004 by
Guild of Master Craftsman Publications Ltd
Castle Place, 166 High Street,
Lewes, East Sussex BN7 1XU

ISBN 1 86108 324 6

A catalogue record for this book is available from the British Library.

Publisher: Paul Richardson
Art Director: Ian Smith
Managing Editor: Gerrie Purcell
Production Manager: Stuart Poole
Editor: Stephen Haynes
Designer: Andy Harrison
Photographer: Anthony Bailey, except as listed on page 6
Illustrator: Simon Rodway

Set in Gill Sans

Colour origination by Icon Reproduction
Printed and bound by Sino Publishing House Ltd, Hong Kong, China

Contents

To my wife Sarah and daughters Eleanor and Hannah, who once again have found that I have not been around much during the writing of this book, but who have encouraged me all the way

Acknowledgements

Thanks to Bert Marsh for his encouragement and help throughout this book, and for writing the Foreword.

Thanks again to Bert Marsh, and to Terry Porter, Chris Stott, John Hunnex, Alan Holtham, Steven Russell, Allan Batty and Gary Rance for their much-valued assistance in supplying pictures and information, or for allowing examples of their work to be included.

I would like to thank the following people for helping me to obtain the relevant timbers for this book:

■ Kirk Boulton and Nick Davidson of Craft Supplies, The Mill, Millers Dale, Nr Buxton, Derbyshire, SK17 8SN (tel: 01298 871636; fax: 01298 872263; email: sales@craft-supplies.co.uk; website: www.craft-supplies.co.uk)

■ Simon Hope of Australian Outback Imports, Unit 4, Rolts Garden Centre, Clacton Road, Elmstead Market, Colchester, Essex, CO7 7DD (tel: 01206 826602; website: www.ozoutbackimports.com)

■ Ken Southall of the International Wood Collectors Society. At the time of writing, the Society has a website at www.woodcollectors.org and can be contacted by email at iwcs@tds.net or by post at 2300 West Rangeline Road, Greencastle, IN 46135-7875, USA.

My thanks to Stephen Haynes, the book's editor. I thought he might have had enough of working with me on my first book; I am so glad that he didn't. As ever, his diligence, dry sense of humour and patience have been greatly appreciated.

Thanks to Andy Harrison for his excellent work in designing this book.

Photographic credits

Photographs in this book are by Anthony Bailey, © GMC Publications Ltd 2004, with the following exceptions: Alan Holtham: pp. 10, 12, 13 (top left, top right, middle right), 14, 15, 18 (bottom), 19 (top), 20 (bottom); Mark Baker: pp. 11, 17, 19 (bottom); Terry Porter: pp. 21, 23; John Hunnex: pp. 31, 33, 57, 61, 63, 65, 73, 79, 81, 85, 105, 109, 117; courtesy of Bert Marsh: pp. 53, 55, 59, 67, 89, 95, 103, 111, 125, 129 (bowl), 150 (bowl), 161 (bowl), 166 (bowl), 172 (bowl); Steven Russell: p. 140 (pecan); Stephen Haynes: frontispiece, pp. 74 (bottom), 177.

Frontispiece
European lime (*Tilia vulgaris*) with burr on trunk

Foreword

I first met Mark Baker a number of years ago, when he watched me at a turning demonstration. I was aware then that he was deeply interested in woodturning, and particularly in what I was turning at that time – maybe hoping to pick up a few crumbs of knowledge! I understand that he was then teaching craftwork; as anyone who has taught will know, while imparting knowledge to others you are constantly learning yourself.

Following his teaching career he worked for a well-known tool company which specialized in developing and making a wide range of woodturning tools and equipment. By this time Mark had become a very competent turner and was regularly demonstrating his skills. Moving on, he took over the editorship of GMC's *Woodturning* magazine, and by dint of enthusiasm and sheer hard work he has impressed his identity on this magazine. Reading his first book, *Woodturning Projects: A Workshop Guide to Shapes*, no one can dispute that he is an extremely good turner and that woodturning is a subject he cares passionately about. Mark's great thirst for knowledge on this subject is always evident; being such a good listener, he knows about the successes and failures that woodturners face, and is always willing to share his own skills and experiences with others.

There has been much discussion of how to raise the standard of woodturning. I am of the opinion that it would improve dramatically if turners would take the trouble to increase their understanding of their material; a greater awareness of the qualities of wood cannot fail to help in both technique and design.

With his extensive knowledge and effective communication skills, Mark has presented a wealth of information in a clear and accessible form. Though the book is slanted towards turners, other wood users will find much of the information extremely valuable.

Congratulations, Mark!

Bert Marsh
July 2004

Introduction

Wood, for many people, has a warmth, a vibrancy and a certain quality that no other material can mimic. We can identify with the growing tree, and the wood from that tree that has been used to make something aesthetically pleasing. Have you noticed that people can rarely resist touching a wooden article?

Turners are in a position to exploit all forms of wood to the fullest. We can use small pieces that others would discard, or massive sections that will either be cut to the sizes we require, or turned into large sculptural forms. We can work with burrs and crotches, with rippled, spalted and quilted pieces; we can even utilize sections with bark inclusions, splits and wormholes. I do not think there is any wood that a turner, given sufficient time and imagination, could not make the most of.

This book is by no means a treatise of turning techniques — there are many fine books available to provide help with that. Nor can a reasonably sized book possibly cover every type of wood available. It does, however, provide a practical guide to over 150 woods from around the world that are suitable for turners.

I have included a wide variety of species which are available from specialist importers and retailers, and all the woods listed are ones that I have turned. A lot of technical data has been published elsewhere, but this is mostly confined to the more readily available timbers, and the information is chiefly aimed at those involved in the construction industry, where considerations of load bearing and

shock resistance are important. Much of this information is irrelevant to turners, which is why this book came about.

I do not profess to be a scientist: like you, I am a turner. I have tried to give information about each wood that is important to turners, such as its name, weight, size, the possible health risks from the dust and the wood itself, and what it looks like. I have added my own practical observations on what the wood feels like to turn. Stephen Haynes, the book's editor, mentioned when reading the descriptions of wood that the terms used reminded him of a journalist describing wine: 'This spalted piece is precocious, bordering on petulant.' This made me laugh, and I realized that his comments were very close to the truth. When describing the colours, I have tried to use terms that will strike a chord with most people, but who is to say that we all view colour in the same way? Some of my comments are bound to be subjective; but hopefully they will serve to indicate what you are likely to encounter in your own turning ventures.

I have listed the common names of each wood, but these vary a lot from place to place and can cause confusion, so I have also included the scientific or Linnaean name, which is usually in Latin or Greek. The advantage of this is that these terms are standardized worldwide so as to identify unambiguously each type of tree, and types that are closely related are placed in family groupings. Most of us do not need to know the full botanical classification, so this book gives only the two most important categories: genus and species. The genus denotes a particular group within the family, and the species is the individual type within the group. Walnut, for instance, is given the generic name of *Juglans*, but the species name will identify exactly what kind of walnut we are talking about: for example, European walnut is *Juglans regia* (genus and species names are always written in italics), while American black walnut is *Juglans nigra*. The wood lists in this book are in alphabetical order according to the Linnaean names, which makes it easier to see which woods are closely related to one another.

I live in England and am fortunate to be in an area with a mild climate. This, of course, has a bearing on how my wood dries and seasons. I am able to rough-turn most of the woods I work (depending on the intended result) and then let them season in my workshop, weighing the wood regularly to monitor the drying process. Some parts of the world are hot and dry, others cold and very dry, and an arid climate will suck the moisture from wood very quickly, probably causing splits. Conversely, those living in areas of high humidity will need to find a way of drying the timber to suit their environment. Please bear in mind when reading this book that I cannot know all the conditions you are likely to encounter, and can only speak in detail of my own situation and the techniques that work here. I mention common drying methods – kilning, air-drying, rough-turning, allowing the wood to dry after it has been turned – which may well work for you. These can form the basis of your approach, but you may

need to modify the procedures to suit your circumstances. Local turners will be able to provide advice.

The pictures in this book show, as far as possible, typical examples of the woods concerned. That said, every piece of wood is different, even when they come from the same tree, and coloration, grain and figuring will all vary. Woods darken or mellow with age and exposure to light, and will change again with the application of a finish – sometimes to a spectacular degree – so when you go and buy a piece of wood it may be quite a bit darker or lighter than the specimen shown. There will also be some colour variations due to the printing and photographic processes used in the book – sadly, there is no way that technology can match the diversity of rich, subtle variations that nature creates. The pictures, though, will provide a good indication of what you are likely to find.

There are timbers in this book from tropical rainforests and from various countries around the world. This should, I hope, raise a lot of questions about their sustainability, and how their extraction can be properly managed, monitored and certified. I do not go into these issues in this book. I will, however, encourage you to be aware of what you are using, and of the potential impact on the environment. I would urge you to explore the timbers that are native to your locality, and learn how to use these to their fullest potential before trying species from further afield, most of which will carry a premium price.

I hope that the information in this book is helpful, and wish you well with your woodturning, wherever it may take you.

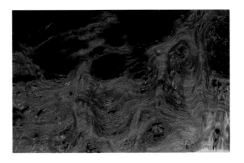

This piece of Australian gimlet burr (*Eucalyptus salubris*) shows how the colour of a piece of wood can be transformed by the use of a finish – in this case oil

Buying wood

We all know that wood is not cheap – especially figured pieces such as burrs, crotches and so on, which carry a price premium. Selecting and buying wood is, to many, a daunting but fascinating experience; the unwary can all too easily be caught out and make expensive mistakes.

Everyone's situation is different: you need to bear in mind how much you can afford, what equipment you have, and where you live. All these factors will affect the size of your workshop and how much storage space is available; and all will have a bearing on the wood you can buy and the projects you can undertake.

Woodyards and specialist timber suppliers offer a wide selection of timber, as do local park and forestry authorities. Tree surgeons are also well worth cultivating. As in most things, it helps to get to know the people we are doing business with – many friendships develop over the years, to mutual benefit. A lot of the wood suppliers I buy from are friends, and will give me a call when they get something special in. Like many woodworkers, I will happily travel many miles for something 'special' – especially when I get the call to say that the wood I have been hunting for has finally arrived.

Experience is the only way to learn how to spot faults and potential problems – just as practice is the only way to get better at turning. Wormholes, for example, may not be visible from outside, and radial splits or shakes may not show either. You are bound to see checks in the ends of the log, but it is difficult to judge how far these extend. Internal areas may be heavily spalted, with only the merest hint of spalting on the end grain. Localized pockets of rot may be hard to spot if the bark is intact. With a figured log, you must decide for yourself how much figuring is likely to be present. It is imperative that we take the time to understand what a piece of wood is truly worth – not only monetarily, but as the raw material of our craft – and how the asking price of the wood relates to the potential value of the finished product.

How to buy

The least expensive way to buy wood is as a log or trunk, or a section thereof. There are a number of problems associated with buying wood in this way, beginning with the cost and time factors involved in transporting it. You need access to the appropriate machinery to cut it to

A stock of waney-edged cherry (*Prunus avium*) boards drying in stick

the required size, and the knowledge of how to convert it to get the maximum yield with the least possible wastage – though wastage during conversion will always be high. Storage is a potential problem, as logs take up a great deal of space; you will also have to season and dry the pieces. You must learn how to spot potential faults such as splits, shakes, rot and so on, which may not be evident from the outside; and also how to recognize areas which may be figured, and to judge how extensive they are likely to be. The plus point is the massive cost saving, compared to buying converted and seasoned timber. However, if you are only turning 20 or so projects a year, or specializing in miniatures or pens, this approach is not likely to be viable or necessary. This way of buying wood is ideal for the professional or semi-professional turner working on a fairly large scale.

The next cheapest method is to buy sawn boards, which are available in various widths and thicknesses depending on the species. Through-and-through-cut boards are the cheapest; the most expensive are planed, dimensioned boards. Either kind can be bought partially seasoned or kiln-dried. When buying wood this way you can see exactly what you are getting, and can pick out the boards you like; you can spot potential faults easily, and you can see the figure. Boards are more convenient to transport and store than logs, and you can more readily cut them into the sections you require. The wood is likely to be partially seasoned, and wastage is reduced. The downside is that because the wood has been worked on at the woodyard, there is a price premium; and because all of the board's surface is visible, the woodyard will be fully aware of any special figuring and will charge you accordingly.

The most expensive way of buying wood is as pre-dimensioned blanks or sections, which are available in a large array of sizes, either partially seasoned or kiln-dried. These are ideally suited for the

A stock of ready-cut blanks for making bowls and hollow forms

amateur who requires only a few pieces in a year, or for those who are after a small piece of something special – a burr, perhaps – for a one-off project. The plus points to buying wood this way are that the pieces are usually planed and sealed so that you can see exactly what you are buying, faults and all; and they can be bought at a size that is close to your requirements, so that storage is easier and takes little space – depending, of course, on how many blanks you keep in stock. Blanks are the most expensive option because the woodyard has converted and dimensioned the logs – thereby incurring wastage – sanded the surface, and possibly also seasoned the wood. Bearing this in mind, maybe they are not that expensive after all.

Storage and handling

Always ensure that there are gaps between the pieces being stored; this will permit airflow and reduce the likelihood of fungal staining and decay. If you have to store pieces on the floor, make sure that it is not damp. If you are unsure about this, place a few wooden stickers on the floor and lay the pieces on this; it is best practice to do this anyway. Please do not be tempted to lift anything that is very heavy on your own – it's surprising how much even small pieces of timber can weigh when wet.

There is not space here for more than a brief outline of the problems involved in choosing wood and preparing it for use. For more detail, consult some of the works listed under **Further Reading** on page 178; I particularly recommend *Wood and How to Dry it*, published by *Fine Woodworking* magazine, and R. Bruce Hoadley's *Understanding Wood*.

A glossary of woodturning terms

Every art, craft or profession uses special words to describe processes, concepts and techniques specific to its own work. These can be very confusing to anyone who has just started out or is looking to enter into the subject. They may represent a real barrier to better understanding. Throughout this book, technical or descriptive terms have been used where appropriate to convey information in an economical way. This glossary is intended to explain them in down-to-earth words and, where necessary, pictures.

A selection of boards being air-dried in stick

air-drying or **air-seasoning** a process in which felled timber – usually after cutting to specific sizes – is placed to dry in the open air, relying on a combination of airflow, atmospheric humidity and the ambient temperature of the surroundings to reduce the moisture content of the wood slowly. Usually the wood is protected from direct sunlight and rain by some form of cover over the top, but the sides are left open to allow the air to pass through unhindered. The pieces are stacked on top of each other, and uniformly sized **sticks** or **stickers** are placed between them at regular intervals to create gaps through which the air can pass; this **stickering** is essential to make sure all the wood is exposed to the drying air. Air-drying can only reduce the moisture content to a limited extent: in the UK, for example, the **equilibrium moisture content** of air-dried timber is deemed to be about 15–20%, depending on the local climate and humidity level.

annual rings or **growth rings** the concentric rings of wood added yearly to the growing tree; in wood from temperate zones these are visibly distinct.

bevel-rubbing tools tools in which the bevel is kept in contact with the wood during the cutting process, and serves as a primary control point of cutting. The main examples are gouges and skew chisels, but parting tools or beading-and-parting tools may also be included, depending on the cutting technique used.

bird's-eye figure figure on the sawn surface of wood that shows many small, rounded, lustrous areas resembling birds' eyes; common in hard or rock maple (*Acer saccharum, A. nigrum*). This is caused by localized grain irregularity, probably due to damage to the **cambial layer**.

blackheart abnormal brown or black discoloration of the heartwood, which is not necessarily decayed. Ash (*Fraxinus* spp.) can be prone to this.

blank a piece of wood that has been cut to a specific size and shape; usually refers to pieces suitable for carving or turning. Buying prepared blanks is undoubtedly the dearest way of acquiring timber; buying planks or boards is cheaper if you have the means to cut them to suitable sizes.

Blister figure in English
elm (*Ulmus procera*)

Bowl by Mark Baker, showing quilted figure
in American soft maple (*Acer saccharinum*)

Irregular figure in English
elm (*Ulmus procera*) burr

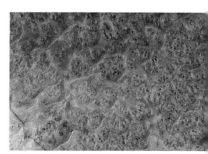

Tightly packed figuring
in amboyna (*Pterocarpus
indicus*) burr

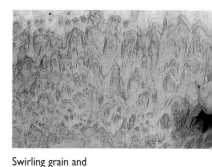

Swirling grain and
pippy knots in York
gum (*Eucalyptus
loxophleba*) burr

blister figure figuring, caused by irregularities in grain direction, which resembles billowing clouds, or sometimes bubble-like forms. If the bubble is ovoid in shape, the term used is **quilting**.

botanical nomenclature we usually refer to woods by their common or local names, such as walnut, ash or jarrah. Much of the time this is adequate, but the names for various types of wood can vary considerably from place to place, and the same name may be used for quite unrelated species. We can avoid confusion by using the system of nomenclature devised by the Swedish botanist Carl Linnaeus. The science of classification, for both plants and animals, is called taxonomy. The full classification for a plant is quite long, but there are usually only two categories that a woodworker need be concerned with: **genus** (plural **genera**) and **species**. The names used are usually in Latin or Greek, but are not that difficult to memorize with a little practice. European walnut, for example, is termed *Juglans regia*, whereas American black walnut is *Juglans nigra*; the first element of the name is the same because both these species belong to the same genus (*Juglans*). Genus and species names are conventionally written in italics, the genus with a capital letter, the species without.

brittleheart heartwood that snaps easily across the grain as a result of compression failure in fibres during growth.

burr (burl) a lumpy, carbuncle-like growth resulting from parasitic attack or damage to the tree, which causes numerous small shoots to develop in that location as the tree grows over the damaged area. The grain orientation in burrs is extremely erratic, yielding some fantastic figuring which varies enormously from piece to piece. Variants include loose, dotted arrangements of small pippy (pip-like) knots amongst contorted, swirling grain; tight, swirling, cloud-like groupings of larger knots; and more tightly packed groupings or clusters of small **pippy** knots.

cambium or **cambial layer** the layer between the sapwood and the inner bark, where new wood is created.

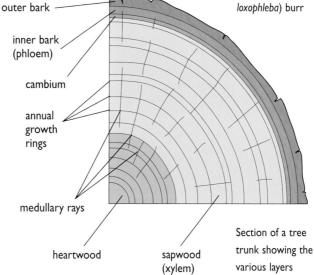

outer bark

inner bark
(phloem)

cambium

annual
growth
rings

medullary rays

heartwood

sapwood
(xylem)

Section of a tree
trunk showing the
various layers

case hardening a defect caused by excessively fast kiln-drying. The surface of the wood dries faster than the core, causing permanent stresses that are released when the wood is cut, resulting in severe distortion.

chatterwork a form of decoration, usually applied to the end grain, made by placing a specially made cutter against the rotating work. Because the blade is quite thin, it vibrates and makes an intermittent cut on the surface. The pattern is affected by the speed of rotation, the pressure of the cutter against the work and the amount of flex there is in the cutter.

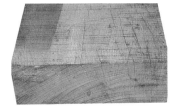

Shallow checks in the end of a sawn board

checks or **checking** cracks running along the grain, caused by uneven or too rapid drying, which creates stresses within the wood that are greater than the latent strength of the wood. In most cases they are not very deep – hence the term **surface checking**.

close-grained having narrow growth rings. This usually indicates that the wood is slow-growing and therefore relatively dense and heavy. Conversely, if the wood is faster-growing the rings will be wider apart and the wood can be described as *open-grained* or *coarse-grained*.

Corrugations on the surface are a symptom of cell collapse

collapse a situation in which the outer layers of the wood dry at a faster rate than the inner parts, creating tension which compresses and distorts the cells of the inner wood. Collapse reveals itself as a corrugated surface on the outside of the wood.

compression wood *see* **reaction wood**

conversion the process of sawing trees or logs into smaller sections in readiness for use. There are several different ways in which a log can be cut. Some methods are very economical from the woodyard's point of view; others produce more

wastage but yield more dimensionally stable timber and, in some species, a more attractive figure.

through and through the log is sawn horizontally along its length, and this is repeated until all of the log has been cut. The boards have a wavy or natural edge running along their length. Another term for this is *slab-sawing*. Wastage is small, but the boards are liable to warp.

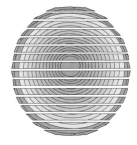

Through-and-through sawing

quartersawing traditionally, boards were cut so as to radiate out from the heart of the tree, much as the spokes of a wheel radiate from the hub. Wood cut in this way is very stable, and in some cases – oak (*Quercus* spp.), for instance – the wood will yield an attractive ray figure.

Traditional quartersawing

Because this method of conversion is expensive and wasteful, an alternative method is now used which is more economical. It still produces the figuring mentioned above, but compromises the dimensional stability of the board a little.

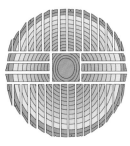

Modern quartersawing

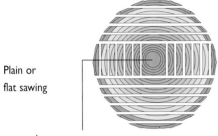

Plain or
flat sawing

heart cut square
and discarded

plain or flat sawing this is similar to through-and-through cutting, apart from the zone that includes the heart of the wood. The heart, because it is unstable, is cut out (*boxed*) and discarded, but the sections to either side of it are cut at a tangent to the grain (*riftsawn*).

crotch (figure) the crotch is the area where a trunk or branch forks. The junction of the two stems creates a localized distortion of the grain which, when cut through along the grain, reveals a very distinctive figure pattern. The method of cutting has a major effect on the appearance of the figuring. If cut in the centre, it yields the normal crotch figure. If cut towards the edge, the figure shown will be what is called **swirl crotch**.

A crotch piece of yew (*Taxus baccata*) seen from the outside

dry weight the dry weight of wood is typically measured at a moisture content of 12%; but take care when comparing figures from different sources, because different criteria may have been used.

Dutch elm disease a fatal disease which affects many species of elm (*Ulmus* spp.) and is caused by the fungi *Ophiostoma ulmi* (syn. *Ceratocystis ulmi*) and the more virulent *O. novo-ulmi*, both spread by elm-bark beetles. The disease is so called because early research on it was carried out in the Netherlands; it is not named after the Dutch elm (*U. hollandica*).

end checks or **end-grain checks** water travels more quickly along the grain than across it, so moisture is lost at a higher rate from the end grain than from any other part of the wood. This area therefore shrinks at a faster rate than the rest, setting up uneven stresses which result in checks (cracks) developing radially in the end grain.

end-rearing storing boards vertically instead of horizontally. Certain woods, such as European sycamore (*Acer pseudoplatanus*), are liable to develop fungal staining if boards are laid flat for seasoning or storage. To avoid this, and to help retain the natural colour of the wood, the timber should be stored on end. The pieces still need to be **stickered** to allow air movement.

equilibrium moisture content wood is hygroscopic: it loses moisture when relative humidity is low, but absorbs water when it is high. There is, however, at any given temperature a point at which no water is lost or taken back: this is the equilibrium moisture content.

extractives substances such as metallic oxides and other chemical compounds deposited in the wood that give it its distinctive colour and resistance to decay.

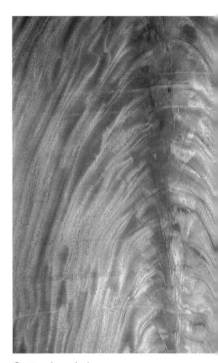

Cutting through the centre of the crotch produces this classic crotch figure

Fiddleback figure in
European sycamore
(*Acer pseudoplatanus*)

fiddleback a figuring caused by wavy grain, in which the fibres of the wood continuously change direction in a regular manner. Fiddleback European sycamore (*Acer pseudoplatanus*) is traditionally used for the backs of violins, but the figuring can occur in other species as well.

figure or **figuring** any decorative pattern on the surface of the wood created by colour variations, faults and defects, growth abnormalities and irregularities, and orientation of the grain. Figuring can be determined by the way the wood is cut, but also by pigment colouring and growth anomalies.

finish-turning the process of creating a finished piece of turned work from a blank that has previously been **rough-turned** and set aside to season and dry further. During the seasoning process the wood will have moved as a result of stress relief and shrinkage, altering the shape of the original rough-turned item. Once the required moisture content has been reached – which can often take many months – the piece can be remounted on the lathe and turned to the shape that you require, then sanded and finished.

flame figure figuring that resembles a flame in appearance.

genus *see* **botanical nomenclature**

girdling the practice of cutting away the bark around the circumference of a tree to cause the tree to die gradually and thereby reduce its moisture content prior to felling. Economic constraints mean that this technique is now rarely used.

grain the arrangement of the fibres in the wood relative to the longitudinal axis of a tree or piece of wood. Many types of grain pattern are distinguished, such as fine, coarse, interlocked, wavy, etc. The word 'grain' tends to refer to the regular pattern of the wood, whereas **figure** refers to interesting irregularities.

green or **unseasoned** wood from trees that have been freshly cut has a very high moisture content and is said to be 'green'.

hardwood wood from a broad-leaved (dicotyledonous) tree. It is usually harder than **softwood**, but not always: balsa (*Ochroma pyramidale*) is a familiar example of a very soft hardwood. The species listed in this book are hardwoods except where otherwise stated.

heart shake a shake that starts at the pith of a log and radiates from there out towards the edge.

heartwood or **true wood** the central part of the trunk, which provides support for the tree. It is the hardest, heaviest and most durable part of the timber, and usually the part of most commercial interest.

heat-checking minute splits, usually in the end grain, caused by heat generated by friction when sanding. Excessive heat may be caused by the application of too much pressure or by using abrasives that are worn out and no longer sharp.

honeycombing or **honeycomb checks** a form of internal damage caused by **case hardening**, which as a result of stress causes the tissues of the timber to break up and form internal checks. These are usually not visible from the outside.

interlocked grain a configuration in which the fibres formed in successive stages of growth are laid down in different orientations. Certain combinations can produce a distinctive figure, such as **ribbon figure**.

in the round a term used to describe a project which uses a whole section of the trunk, bough or limb of a tree, rather than a previously prepared **blank**.

kiln drying a process that uses a heated chamber, operated by gas, electric or solar power, to dry the wood to a predetermined moisture content. Some woods need to be air-dried before they are kilned, to prevent degrade; others can be kilned immediately after conversion from the log. The best results are obtained when the pieces in the kiln are of a uniform size or thickness; otherwise each piece will respond differently and dry at different rates. Each species of wood requires a specific drying regime in order to produce stable timber that does not degrade during drying.

liming traditionally, a process in which the grain of an open-grained wood such as oak or ash (*Quercus, Fraxinus* spp.) was filled with a lime slurry which set in the wood's pores. Once dry, this was sanded back to reveal the natural colour of the wood on the surface, leaving the filled pores a distinctive milky-white colour. Nowadays, tinted paste waxes of various colours, including white, are used to create a similar visual contrast, but the traditional term is still used.

medullary rays sheets of tissue formed at right angles to the annual rings of the tree. In some species, such as oak (*Quercus* spp.), they are very distinctive; in others they are barely visible. How the wood is cut will have a big bearing on how these show on the cut timber. Quartersawing displays the medullary rays to great visual effect on oak and other timbers.

moisture content (MC) the moisture content of wood varies a lot depending on whether the wood is green (wet) or seasoned (dry). The way to tell is by weighing it. The completely dry (**oven-dry**) weight of a given species of wood is a constant, and the moisture content of the wood at any given moment can be expressed as a percentage of this constant. The formula is:

MC = weight of water present in sample ÷ oven-dry weight of sample × 100

mottle ripple figuring that has been broken up by interlocking grain. It is in effect a broken stripe figure with irregular interruptions caused by the wavy grain.

movement a general term for the various ways in which wood shrinks and distorts as it seasons, due to moisture loss or the relief of inherent stresses within the wood.

An example of distortion in a rough-turned bowl, which will subsequently be finish-turned to a regular shape

Natural-edged bowl in European maple (*Acer campestre*) burr by Mark Baker

natural-edge work any piece of work which retains part of the natural, unadulterated outer surface of the tree, often including the bark, to create visual contrast with the 'finished' surface.

partially seasoned not fully dried. More often than not this refers to air-dried wood, but it may apply to any wood that has not been seasoned or dried to the moisture content required for the place in which it will eventually be situated. In the UK, for example, air-dried wood often has a moisture content of 17% or higher, depending on how long it has been cut and stored, whereas the average moisture content in a centrally heated room is 10–12%. Any wood whose moisture content exceeds that of its immediate environment is deemed to be partially seasoned, and is liable to show **movement**.

penetrative finish any finish which penetrates the fibres of the wood and protects it – typically oils of various types, or some paste or liquid waxes. The finish may not set – some natural oils do not contain drying agents – but may still provide an effective barrier against moisture ingress, dirt and chemicals. Modern proprietary oil finishes combine natural oils with synthetic elements to increase the protection, and may incorporate dryers which will cause the penetrative finish to set and form a protective surface film in addition to the usual physical barrier. The degree of penetration depends on the density of the wood; with very dense woods such as lignum vitae (*Guaiacum officinale*) they do not penetrate far at all, but still form an effective finish. Multiple coats are required to obtain a fine finish. Oils without dryers can be retouched whenever necessary; those with dryers must be sanded back before applying a fresh coat.

pigment staining not all figuring is caused by irregularities within the grain. Colours within wood, such as the stripes in ebony (*Diospyros* spp.), are caused by **extractives** within the heartwood which have coloured the wood.

A striking example of pigmented striping in ebony (*Diospyros* sp.)

pippy a term used to describe a burr pattern in which numerous small knots – 'eyes' or 'pips' – are present in a clustered or loosely spaced arrangement.

pluck-out or **pull-out** the situation in which the tool pulls a clump of fibres away from the main body of the wood, resulting in a serious blemish which can run very deep. It often occurs when the wood has decayed a little and lost some of its strength, so the fibres are not so tightly bonded together as they were.

possible health risks many substances can cause allergic reactions in certain individuals, who may not be aware of the risk until they actually come into contact with the substance in question. Sometimes the effects are cumulative. Long-term exposure to dust can have serious effects on lung function, or result in conditions such as contact dermatitis; other reactions may be caused by chemical compounds in the wood. The possible risks mentioned in this book have been gathered from health and safety bodies around the world, and from anecdotal comments. Most published research has been done on readily available species, which is why anecdotal evidence has had to be included for many woods which are only available in small amounts and have not been the subject of systematic study. *All* dust is potentially hazardous: take sensible precautions to limit exposure to it, and take a shower afterwards to ensure that the dust is not in contact with your skin any longer than necessary. Be careful also of the finishes that you use: these can contain harmful chemicals.

power sanding for this you need an arbor with a hook-and-loop face onto which is affixed abrasive, and a method of driving it, such as a drill. The revolving arbor is traversed across the surface of the work as it turns slowly on the lathe. Best results are achieved by having the arbor run in contra-rotation to the work. Power sanding is devilishly quick, and a light touch is required so as not to create furrows.

Power-sanding arbors fitted with abrasive discs

quartersawing *see* **conversion**

quilting *see* **blister figuring**

radial crack this happens when the tangential shrinkage in a trunk, log or branch generates stresses which the wood cannot withstand, so that it splits along the grain. These cracks are usually very deep and can penetrate right to the heart of the tree. It is not uncommon to find more than one, starting from different positions.

Radial cracks are very evident in this log

radial surface a wood surface cut at right angles to the annual rings, as when a log is sawn through its centre. It seldom shows interesting grain patterning, except in woods which exhibit **ray fleck** or **ribbon figure**. Surfaces cut at an angle to the annual rings are described as **tangential**.

Radial, tangential and transverse surfaces

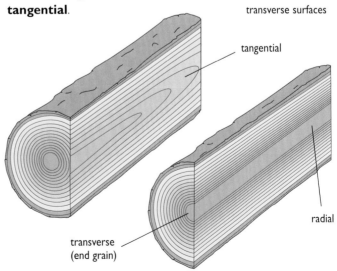

tangential

radial

transverse (end grain)

Conspicuous ray fleck in European oak (*Quercus petraea* or *Q. robur*)

ray fleck part of a **medullary ray** showing on a radial surface; usually regarded as a decorative feature, especially in oak (*Quercus* spp.).

reaction wood an area of wood on a branch or a leaning trunk which shows distinctive characteristics because of the tensions and pressures due to gravity. It is denser but much more brittle than normal wood. In hardwoods it generally occurs on the upper side of the branch or trunk, and is called **tension wood**; on softwoods it forms on the underside and is known as **compression wood**.

relative humidity the amount of moisture currently held in the air, expressed as a percentage of the amount which the air would hold when fully saturated at the same temperature.

ribbon figure a type of figuring produced as a result of **interlocking grain**. It only shows when the wood has been cut radially.

Ribbon figure in African walnut (*Lovoa trichilioides*)

ring failure or **ring shake** a separation of the wood fibres, occurring parallel to and between the annual rings in the growing tree.

ripple figure another name for **fiddleback** figure.

roe or **roey figure** short, broken stripe or **ribbon figure** in certain quartersawn hardwoods, arising from interlocked grain interrupting a ribbon figure.

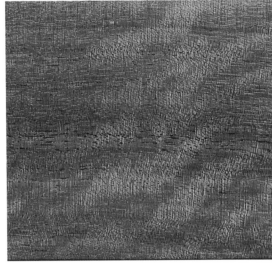

Typical roe figure on radial surface of Queensland maple (*Flindersia brayleyana*)

rough-turning a technique used to ensure that wood is fully seasoned or dried, so that movement will be minimal in the final piece. When wood — especially air-dried wood — is turned from the solid, the inside is rarely dry, and is therefore likely to suffer from some shrinkage. Furthermore, the removal of the central core will release some of the stresses inherent in the wood, which is likely to twist a little — or a lot, depending on the species. In rough-turning, the external profile is first turned to approximately the required shape. The piece is then reversed on the lathe and turned on the inside, but the wall thickness is deliberately left thicker than normal to take account of the movement that is likely to occur. The ratio

I work to is 1in (25mm) wall thickness per 12in (300mm) diameter, or, alternatively, a wall thickness equal to 10% of the overall diameter. However, some woods which suffer from high shrinkage may require a more generous allowance, as noted in the alphabetical entries. The internal wall profile is usually turned to match the external profile, at least approximately; if the shape is too different and the wall thickness is not even, differential shrinkage rates are likely to cause splits. Moisture is lost fastest through the end grain, and if you live in a hot or arid environment you may find the wood drying out too fast, in which case coating the rough-turned piece with PVA adhesive will help to retard and even out the drying process. (Bert Marsh first introduced me to this highly effective technique.) An alternative approach is to seal the rough-turned piece in a plastic bag. Every two or three days, take the piece out, turn the bag inside out, and reseal. This creates a very controlled humidity level and ensures slow drying.

sapwood the softer, less durable, less dense wood towards the outer surface of the trunk, confined in most species to a narrow band in relation to the heartwood. It is not always easily distinguished from the heartwood.

seasoning the process by which 'stable' timber is created. This entails reducing the moisture content, but also relieving the inherent stresses in the wood so as to minimize the likelihood of movement when it is placed in the environment in which it is to be used. Dry wood is more dimensionally stable than wet (green) timber. Strength, hardness and stiffness are increased by up to 50% over that of green wood.

sensitizer any substance which, after initial exposure, will invariably cause an allergic reaction in the user when encountered again. In the case of some wood species, this reaction may take the form of dermatitis, other skin disorders, or respiratory and associated problems.

shake a serious split in a piece of wood, which is not necessarily a result of the drying stresses.

shear-scraping a cutting technique in which a scraper, or the edge of a gouge, is presented at such an angle to the work as to cause shavings to peel off the cutting edge. There is no bevel rub during this cut. A good angle to begin with is 45°, with the tool trailed across the surface of the rotating work. The angle of approach can be varied: if you find that 45° is not right and you are tearing the wood, lessen or increase the angle until you achieve a fine peeling cut. The object is to clean up the surface and minimize the need for sanding with coarse grades.

Shear-scraping with the face of the tool (in this case a specialized shear scraper with interchangeable tips) presented in a trailing mode at 45° to the work

silver grain the figure created by lustrous **ray fleck** on quartersawn timber, especially oak (*Quercus* spp.).

softwood wood from a coniferous (gymnosperm) tree. It is generally softer than **hardwood**, but not always; yew (*Taxus* spp.) is a good example of a very hard softwood.

sp., spp. abbreviations for **species**, singular and plural. 'Quercus sp.' means 'an unspecified or unidentified species of the genus Quercus'; 'Quercus spp.' means 'various species of the genus Quercus'.

spalted wood wood that has been invaded by fungi, which produce various colour changes as they progress. When the colour changes occur without drastically reducing the inherent strength of the wood, the material is said to be spalted. This wood is, in effect, in the primary stages of rot. The same term is sometimes used for timber that is in a more advanced state of decay.

Characteristic spalting pattern in European beech (Fagus sylvatica)

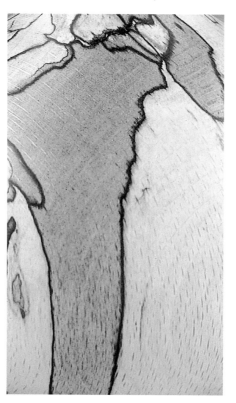

species see **botanical nomenclature**

specific gravity (SG) a measure of the density of a substance relative to that of water. Anything with a specific gravity of more than 1.0 is heavier than water, and sinks when placed in it; an example is satiné bloodwood (Brosimum paraense), which has a specific gravity of 1.15. Specific gravity may vary considerably from one specimen to another of the same species, and the figures given in this book can only be regarded as averages.

sticks or **stickers** pieces of wood of uniform size that are placed between horizontally stacked boards to support them and allow air to flow between them. Such boards are said to be in **stick** or **stickered**.

stump the base section of the tree, just above and just below ground level. This can exhibit some interesting figuring.

surface checking see **checks**

surface finish any finish which does not deeply penetrate the wood, but forms a chemical or physical bond with the wood surface and provides a protective film or a base on which other finishes can be applied. Lacquers, shellac-based finishes (friction polish and French polish), varnishes of all types, hard block waxes and so on are some of the surface finishes available. Invariably they will require more than one coat to form an effective finish or base.

synonym or **syn.** scientific names of plants are occasionally changed, as botanists revise their ideas of the relationships between individual species and genera. A synonym, in this sense of the word, is a botanical name that is no longer current in scientific use, but may still be found in older textbooks or in less scholarly sources.

tangential surface see **radial surface**

tear-out a surface blemish caused when the fibres of the grain are broken or torn away from the surrounding fibres. It tends to occur when cutting against the grain, or where there are grain irregularities such as wavy or interlocking grain.

tension wood *see* **reaction wood**

ultraviolet (UV) inhibitors additives included in certain finishes to block or retard ultraviolet light, which is the primary cause of colour degrade within wood. They act in the same way as sunblocks applied to the skin.

wane or **waney edge** the natural edge of a plank or board, which may be irregular and have bark on it.

wet sanding a sanding technique which employs a lubricant. I first saw it used by Ray Key, who applies paste wax to the finish-turned piece prior to sanding with fine abrasive. The dust and wax combine to form a slurry which gets pushed into the grain and acts as a grain filler. No further finishing is required, other than burnishing with a clean cloth. Oil or water can also be used as lubricants; I mostly use oil. Simply turn the work to the required profile and dry-sand any major blemishes away. Then apply a coat of oil or wax to the surface, and sand at a low speed. If you see dust forming, you need to apply more lubricant and work through the grades of abrasive. After sanding, use a clean cloth to apply a further coat of the oil or wax, then burnish to a smooth finish. One drawback is that this method can only be used when the wood colour is uniform: on a wood such as laburnum (*Laburnum anagyroides*) which has cream sapwood and dark heartwood, the sanding slurry will be dark and will contaminate the lighter sapwood.

wet turning turning freshly cut or unseasoned wood. Wet timber is very enjoyable to turn – large shavings and a lot of water are produced instead of chippings and dust – but the item should be turned to a thin, even wall thickness to reduce the likelihood of splitting. Excessive or uneven thickness will cause differential drying rates across the work, and the resulting tension and stress is likely to cause splits.

woolly grain a fuzzy surface with frayed, rather than cleanly cut, fibres after cutting, resembling a mild form of tear-out. Certain woods, such as the willows (*Salix* spp.), are very susceptible, especially when turned wet.

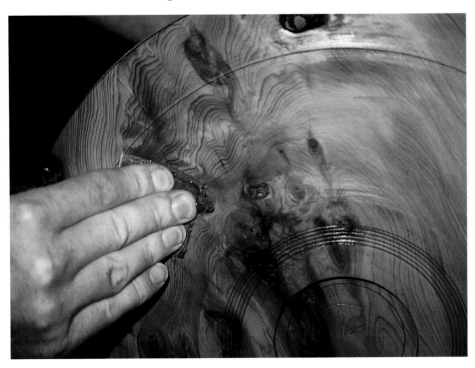

Wet-sanding by hand, in this case using sunflower oil as the lubricant

"To touch, smell and craft wood is a pleasure realized by few but admired by many"

50 woods in detail

European maple

Acer campestre

Other names

Field maple. Norway maple (*A. platanoides*) and Bosnian maple (*A. platanus*) are very similar and are also marketed as 'European maple'

Burr (burl)

Grows

UK, mainland Europe, USA and parts of Asia

Height 60–65ft (18–20m)

Trunk diameter 1–2ft (0.3–0.6m)

Specific gravity .69

Typical dry weight 43lb/ft³ (690kg/m³)

Seasoning

European maple exhibits little degrade or movement when air-dried slowly; however, rapid but careful kiln-drying is recommended (despite the slightly increased risk of movement) to preserve the creamy-white colour. Rough-turned pieces will not distort too much during the drying and stabilizing process, but this is dependent on the amount of figuring in the piece: the more figuring, the higher the potential for distortion. With crotch figuring, as with most highly figured areas of wood, there is a risk of splitting unless it is dried slowly. Try coating the rough-turned piece with PVA to slow the drying process. Kiln-dried wood is fine for furniture and joinery components.

Description

Acers are wonderful woods to work with, and no turner should ignore them. A wide range of figured forms is available, and the uses to which the wood can be put are endless. The heartwood of field maple is creamy-white at first, but will mellow to a light tan colour with time. The sapwood is usually not distinguishable from the heartwood. The grain is normally straight but occasionally wavy or curly, with a fine, even texture. The grain pattern is delicate but clearly defined. Occasionally it will form ripple or curly figure; both of these are highly prized in the veneer trade, and heavily figured trees are usually snapped up very quickly, but turners may come across areas of figure in boards and precut blanks. This wood regularly produces burrs (burls), which more often than not comprise tightly packed clusters of small pippy knots.

Field maple is only available in small to medium sizes, so it is generally more suitable for smaller projects such as bowls or hollow forms, rather than platters. It is often overlooked in favour of more flashy, brightly coloured woods. Being fine-grained, it is suitable for architectural, artistic, decorative and utilitarian work, including items which may come into contact with food. The burrs are wonderful for natural-edge work.

Working qualities

Acers are a large genus with over 100 species. Because there are so many, acers are available commercially in many countries, and form the backbone of many turners' wood requirements. Field maple, along with rock maple (A. saccharum and A. nigrum) and soft maple (A. rubrum and A. saccharinum), is a beautiful wood to work with and a good one to develop your turning skills on. It is a fine-grained, medium-density wood that will hold quite fine detail. It has a slight blunting effect on cutting edges, but cuts well with both hand and machine tools. It will steam-bend, so can be used for making chair backs. It is an ideal timber for kitchen utensils.

It cuts cleanly with sharp tools, but you may experience a little grain tear-out when working highly figured areas, especially with scrapers. During turning it is easy to see from the finish off the tool whether the optimum cut is being achieved, and whether the tool is sharp. With care, it is possible to get a surface finish that requires very little sanding.

This is also an ideal timber for wet turning. Turn the piece to a thin, even wall thickness, apply your finish of choice, then let it dry. As it dries it will 'move' and distort — more so if there is figure in it — to create a highly individual piece. Burrs, natural-edged or not, respond well to this technique. The burr when dry may take on a distinctive texture with a sort of 'hammered' quality to it.

European maple takes finishes well, but the creamy-white colour of the freshly cut wood will be lost unless a finish with a light inhibitor is used. Oils and many surface finishes, such as shellac and lacquers, will have a slight darkening effect. The wood also takes dye well, to highlight the grain and figuring.

Field maple responds well to wet sanding, but can also be sanded dry. Follow this by buffing with a power buff loaded with a fine abrasive compound, which will bring out its wonderful, natural silky lustre.

Hint
Work with freshly honed tools for the final cuts to create a surface that requires very little sanding

Bowl in burr maple by Mark Baker, finished with lemon oil

Boxelder

Acer negundo

Other names
Ashleaf maple, Manitoba maple, maple, red river maple, cut-leaf maple

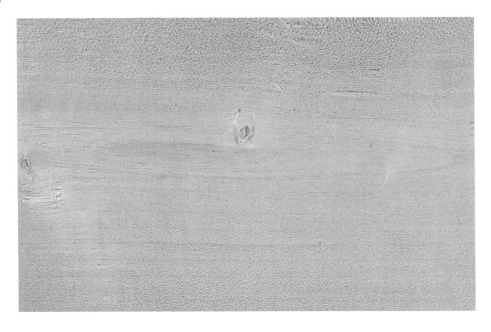

Example with red pigmentation

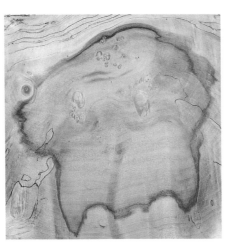

Grows
Canada and USA
Height 60–65ft (18–20m)
Trunk diameter 1ft–3ft 6in (0.3–1.1m)
Specific gravity .45
Typical dry weight 28lb/ft^3 (450kg/m^3)

Seasoning

Boxelder dries with little degrade whether kiln- or air-dried, and is stable in use when seasoned properly. As with most woods, when the work is required to maintain its shape it is best to rough-turn the wood and then put it aside for some time to stabilize. It can, however, be wet-turned to completion and allowed to move so as to produce more 'organic' forms – but the amount of movement is very variable. If the wood is air-dried or stored for too long, blue staining may occur, and the results are often disappointing: muddy, greyish puddles or thin threads, rather than clearly difined bands or lines of colour.

Description

Boxelder is a lightweight, porous but close-grained wood with a fine texture. It tends to have yellow-brown heartwood and green-tinged yellow sapwood. It does not have a clearly defined grain figure, and its blandness may make it ideal for carvers, and for turners who add carved decoration. However, it sometimes has a wavy or curly figuring, which lifts its appearance no end. But it is most highly prized when it has pink or deep red-purple streaks running through it, possibly caused by fungal activity. When there is a lot of this colouring present, boxelder takes on a whole new persona, blossoming from a dull also-ran into a glorious diva. Have you guessed that I like this form of boxelder? It is chiefly used for artistic or decorative work – hollow forms with red streaking look stunning.

Working qualities

Boxelder has a medium blunting effect on cutting edges and cuts reasonably well, although the figured areas may pluck out even if the tools are ultra-sharp. It cuts best with bevel-rubbing tools (gouges and skew chisels). Being soft, it does not hold fine detail well. It can be used for wet turning.

The wood is somewhat soft in any case, but areas of colouring can be softer still, and care is needed when sanding, since aggressive sanding of the soft pockets may create humps in the surface. A light, delicate touch is all that is needed. When working with coloured timber, dry-sand only, to avoid colour contamination.

Being a porous wood, boxelder can be hungry as far as finishes are concerned, requiring a few extra coats of surface or penetrative finish in order to build up a lustrous, silky surface. Dyes can be used to good effect to bring out the wavy or curly figuring on samples without the fungal staining.

Hint

Prior to making the final cuts, apply two or three coats of thinned-down pre-catalysed lacquer or sanding sealer and allow to dry. This hardens the wood a little, which makes the final finishing cuts and sanding easier, minimizing the risk of a bumpy surface

Bowl by Mark Baker, finished with satin lacquer

European sycamore
Acer pseudoplatanus

Other names
Sycamore plane, great maple, plane (in Scotland). Not related to American sycamore (*Platanus occidentalis*), which is of the plane family

Ripple or fiddleback figure (clear varnish finish)

Possible health risks
Not known

Grows
UK, mainland Europe, western Asia; now also planted in USA
Height 100ft (30m)
Trunk diameter 5ft (1.8m)
Specific gravity .61
Typical dry weight 38lb/ft³ (610kg/m³)

Seasoning
The wood seasons well, whether kiln- or air-dried. When air-drying, the boards must be stood on end ('end-reared') to prevent staining. Rapid kilning will help preserve the natural creamy colour. If the wood is laid horizontally and stickered, it will develop a silvery colour with green- or blue-tinged blotches; these are water and fungal stains, and can look quite attractive. This form is known as 'weathered sycamore'. A coloured form known as **harewood** is created artificially, using dyes to colour kiln-dried wood; this gives a wonderful translucent silver colour.

Rough-turning will create very stable wood: there is a moderate amount of movement, but the usual guideline of 1in (25mm) of wall thickness for every 12in (300mm) of diameter still applies.

Description

A wonderful timber to work with, sycamore is creamy-white to yellowish-white in colour; the sapwood is not readily distinguishable from the heartwood. On exposure to light, the wood will darken to a tan or fawn colour. The grain is typically close and straight, but may have curly or lacy figuring. The characteristic ripple or fiddleback figure is highly sought-after by violin makers and veneering companies, who snap up highly figured trees as soon as they become available, so you are more likely to encounter this type of figuring in small amounts – unless you know of a particularly helpful tree surgeon who will tell you when a suitable tree is coming down. Sycamore has a fine, even texture, is of medium density and will hold detail well. Available in large sizes, this is an excellent wood for large platters and hollow forms, as well as smaller projects. It is a valuable wood for furniture turnery and baluster spindles, and is extensively used by cabinetmakers.

Working qualities

Sycamore is a wonderful timber to use in many different woodworking disciplines. I prefer it to field maple (*A. campestre*). It is to my mind a bit of a shrinking violet: it does not shout 'Look at me!', but has an understated beauty that really shines when lovingly finished.

The wood cuts well and holds reasonably fine detail, which can prove useful for pieces that are to be carved or sculpted. Its close grain makes it ideal for use on items that will come into contact with food. Any ripple sections can be somewhat problematic if the cuts are too heavy-handed or if tools are dull. I know this is true of most woods, but gentle cuts with sharp tools will minimize grain tear-out. Sycamore responds better to shear-scraping than to conventional scraping. It can be sanded wet or dry, and accepts surface and penetrative finishes well.

Because it is prone to movement as it dries, this is a great timber with which to experiment with wet turning; flared rims, for example, will distort into interesting wavelike forms. Natural-edged vases, hollow forms and bowls are all worth trying. Since it is available in large sizes, there is plenty of scope to explore the full potential of this timber.

Hint
Small areas of figuring on hollow forms can be highlighted to wonderful effect using dyes, which will be absorbed unevenly by the figured wood

Semi-enclosed form by John Hunnex

Soft maple
Acer rubrum and *A. saccharinum*

Other names
Red maple,
Carolina red
maple,
Drummond
red maple,
scarlet maple,
silver maple

Ambrosia figure

Grows
Canada and eastern USA
Height 60–100ft (18–30m)
Trunk diameter 2ft 6in (0.8m)
Specific gravity *A. rubrum* .63,
A. saccharinum .55
Typical dry weight *A. rubrum*
39lb/ft³ (630kg/m³), *A. saccharinum*
34lb/ft³ (550kg/m³)

Quilted figure

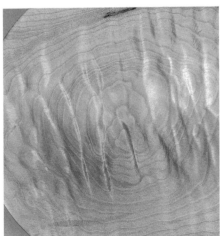

**Possible
health
risks**
Dust may
affect lung
function

Burr (burl)

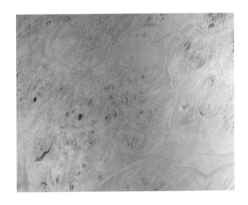

Description

This medium-density wood has light to dark reddish-brown heartwood which may be faintly tinted with purple, grey or green. Usually straight and close-grained, it can occasionally be wavy or curly. Quilting and burr forms are available from time to time. Very attractive pith flecks may be present. The sapwood varies from white to greyish-white. Heavily figured trees are bought for veneers. This wood is sometimes attacked by ambrosia beetles, and fungal spores colonize the tracks left by the beetle to form some wonderful coloured patterns, each piece of course unique. This is known as **ambrosia maple**.

Working qualities

This wood has many uses within the woodworking industry; because it works easily, it is valuable to turners for utility objects such as kitchenware, as well as artistic and decorative pieces, cabinetry and joinery work; it is also suitable for carving. It responds well to wet turning.

Although not as durable and hard-wearing as rock maple (*A. saccharum*, *A. nigrum*), the sheer variety of forms available makes this a very interesting timber indeed. I love the quilted and ambrosia-figured wood especially. To show off the figure and colour to the fullest, I like to use the ambrosia maple on hollow forms and the quilted maple on platters or bowls. Straight-grained soft maple cuts easily and finishes well, but the quilted or curly-grained pieces, due to their erratic grain structure, can be a little difficult to work. Sharp tools and gentle cuts will help a lot, but shear-scraping is recommended, rather than conventional scraping, after the cuts with a gouge. Do not be tempted to skip grades of abrasive on this wood – or any others, come to think of it. Little areas of imperfection have a nasty habit of showing up only after oiling or finishing, making it necessary to backtrack to the abrading stages again.

All forms, except the ambrosia maple, respond well to wet or dry sanding. Because of the risk of colour contamination during wet sanding, ambrosia maple is best sanded dry. Soft maple can be finish-hungry, so three to four coats may be necessary to build up a fine finish. Power buffing is effective to enhance what is already a fine timber and create a silky lustre.

Natural-topped hollow form in burr maple by John Hunnex

Rock maple

Acer saccharum and *A. nigrum*

Other names

Hard maple, sugar maple, white maple (*A. saccharum*); black maple, black sugar maple, hard rock maple (*A. nigrum*). Both species are sold as 'hard' or 'rock' maple

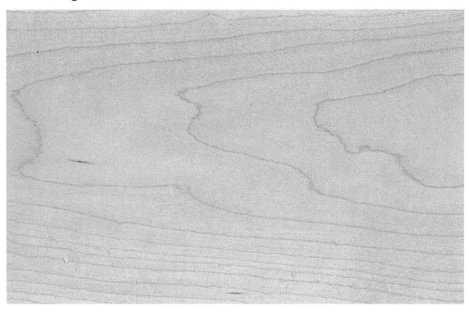

Ripple figure

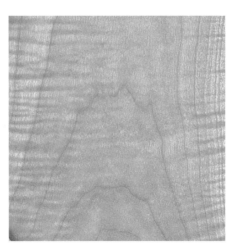

Grows

Canada and USA

Height *A. saccharum* 70–120ft (20–37m), *A. nigrum* 80ft (24m)

Trunk diameter 2–3ft (0.6–0.9m)

Specific gravity .72

Typical dry weight 45lb/ft³ (720kg/m³)

Bird's-eye figure

! Possible health • risks
Dust may affect lung function

Seasoning

The wood dries slowly but is easy to season. It is classified as having a medium to high shrinkage rate and moderate tendency to warp. It responds very well to rough-turning before further seasoning, which is especially necessary with highly figured pieces; the rule of 1in (25mm) of wall thickness to every 12in (300mm) diameter, or 10% of the overall diameter, should be enough to cope with the likely degree of movement.

Description

This beautiful timber is dense, close-grained and tough. The sapwood is white to cream in colour, with a red tinge. The heartwood is typically a uniform light tan to reddish-brown, with a nice pronounced grain pattern. It usually has a straight, tight, fine-textured grain that holds detail well without break-out. These are the maples that produce the most highly figured variant forms, namely rippled or fiddleback, blister, leaf, burr, bird's-eye and occasionally quilted. **Bird's-eye maple** comprises a creamy-white background covered with small, brown, eye-shaped dots. The burr forms can range from tight clusters of pippy dots through to swirling grain and striated patterns. The rock maples, being considerably harder than the soft maples, are highly sought-after, and have myriad uses within the woodworking industry.

Working qualities

Rock maple is certainly one of the gems of the maple family. The variety of figured variants can keep many turners busy for a lifetime. This dense, tight-grained timber is a delight to work with. It cuts well: even the highly figured forms respond well to a sharp tool and a light touch, yielding a finish that requires very little abrading. Its ability to hold detail means that it can be used for complex turned work, and it can be wet-turned to good effect. It is hard-wearing (it is used for flooring, squash courts and industrial rollers), so will stand up to arduous use in utilitarian articles such as chopping boards, pestles and mortars, or salad bowls, as well as being suitable for decorative or artistic work, cabinetry and joinery components.

The warm colour is enhanced further with a nice finish, oil being my favourite; but this depends very much on its intended use. It also accepts surface finishes. A very fine finish is achieved using the wet sanding technique.

Rock maple is available in large sizes, and the varieties of dramatic figuring will constantly amaze. If you have not had the pleasure of trying this wood, please do: I know you will enjoy the experience.

Hint

A freshly honed scraper, used gently, will produce nice delicate ribbons of shavings; this is a useful way to remove any minor ripples left after using a gouge, without tearing out the grain prior to sanding

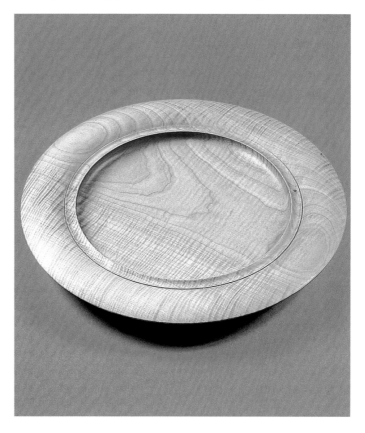

Platter in ripple maple by Mark Baker

Horse chestnut

Aesculus hippocastanum

Other names
European horse chestnut. Also colloquially known in the UK as 'conker tree', after the game called 'conkers' played with the fruit of the tree

Grows
UK and mainland Europe; related species grown in the USA include **buckeye** (*A. glabra* and other spp.)
Height 70–100ft (21–34m)
Trunk diameter 2ft (0.6m)
Specific gravity .51
Typical dry weight 31lb/ft³ (510kg/m³)

Description
The heartwood is normally creamy-white to yellow, with little or no demarcation between heart and sapwood. Winter-felled wood tends to be white, but that felled at other times can vary from yellow to light brown. It has a fine, close, uniform texture with a delicate grain pattern. Horse chestnut can be cross-, spiral- or wavy-grained, and ripple or mottled figuring on longitudinal surfaces is not uncommon. It is also prone to forming burrs.

Seasoning
Horse chestnut dries quickly with little degrade, and can be air- or kiln-dried. It is, however, liable to distortion and end-splitting, and blue stain may occur if it is stored incorrectly. Rough-turning is definitely recommended, especially for burrs (burls). Weigh the rough-turned wood periodically: when it ceases to lose weight, it is ready to turn.

Possible health risks
Not known

Working qualities

Horse chestnut has a moderate dulling effect on cutting edges, and cuts well when freshly seasoned. Figured wood is a good candidate for wet turning. It is a relatively light wood and, despite having a fine grain structure, does not hold fine detail well. Old pieces can be very dry, producing a lot of dust when turning, and may be liable to grain pluck-out.

If stored in damp conditions, the wood may be prone to fungal attack. A small amount of fungal staining may add interest, but if it goes too far and becomes rot it will seriously weaken this already soft wood, making it extremely tedious to work, with constant grain pull-out.

Being easy to work, horse chestnut has a variety of uses in the woodworking industry (cabinetmaking, interior construction and so on), but I think this bland-looking timber is best reserved for turning which is to be carved or sculpted, for which I find it very good. This does not apply to burred or figured pieces: these features really make the wood come alive. The burrs in particular are fantastic to work with.

Though horse chestnut works wonderfully when wet, it can be a little problematic when seasoned, as it is prone to grain tear-out when scrapers are used. It is best to use bevel-rubbing tools and then go straight to abrasives to remove any minor blemishes. Horse chestnut abrades well with the dry sanding method. It finishes well (though it can be a little 'hungry'), and can be dyed to good effect. I find that a surface finish such as pre-catalysed lacquer is the most effective way to highlight the grain and figure.

Hint
Try to get a fine finish straight from the gouge, followed by sanding to remove any minor imperfections. Scraping will cause grain tear-out.

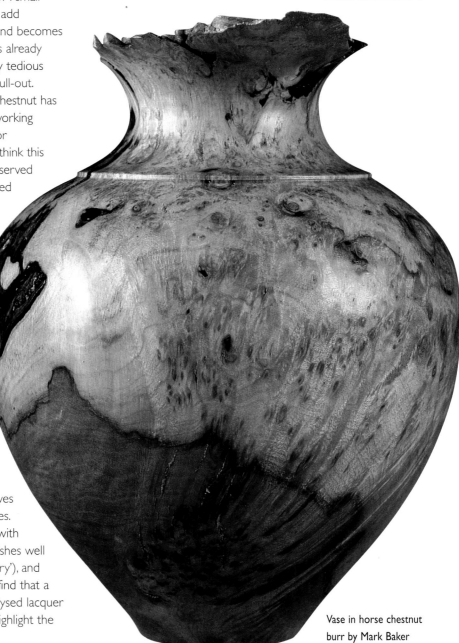

Vase in horse chestnut burr by Mark Baker

Madrona

Arbutus menziesii

Other names
Strawberry tree, pacific madrone, coast madrone, arbutus, manzanita, madroño, jarrito

Burr (burl)

Possible health risks
Not known

Grows
Canada and USA
Height 20–80ft (6–24m)
Trunk diameter 2–3ft (0.6–0.9m)
Specific gravity .77
Typical dry weight 48lb/ft³ (770kg/m³)

Seasoning
This wood is difficult to dry. The very high moisture content of freshly cut wood can result in cell collapse, warping, excessive shrinking and checking as the wood dries. The shrinkage will be uneven, especially in burrs (burls). The best option in my opinion is to turn it while wet to an even, very thin wall thickness – say ⅛in (3mm) or less. The wood's tendency to shrink and warp can be exploited to maximum effect with these thin wet turnings that are designed to move as the wood dries. Do, however, maintain an even wall thickness throughout, or you will very likely experience splitting due to differential drying and contraction rates. Rough-turning may work, but allow extra wall thickness and coat the piece with PVA to even out the drying. Even then, this method has a very high failure rate.

Description

The light pink to pale red-brown heartwood can sometimes have red spots in it. The grain is fine, and may be either straight or irregular, with a smooth, uniform texture. Growth rings within the wood may form unusual, irregular patterns that can be particularly attractive. The sapwood is whitish or sometimes cream, and may have a pink tinge. The burrs (burls) can be a riot of colour, ranging from creams through to vivid scarlet tints, with a variety of figuring, from swirling grain to knot clusters.

Not only the main trunk, but the branches and even the root system can be used, and the figuring and colour of root wood can be quite spectacular. These gnarled root forms are particularly prized by sculptors.

Working qualities

This medium-density timber is a dream to work with when green. There will be long ribbons of shavings coming off the gouge, which is always a pleasant experience. Using scrapers on wet wood can be a little tricky, but light cuts with sharp tools will be OK.

Madrona is also pleasant to work when freshly seasoned and dried, cutting cleanly with most tools but giving best results when bevel-rubbing tools are used. Old wood, however, may give rise to a great deal of dust. Areas of irregular grain require light cuts with a sharp tool to minimize grain pluck-out.

Seasoned wood sands well using either the wet or the dry sanding method. When turning wet, I recommend a wet-sanding method using water as a lubricant. After sanding, let the wood dry, and then give it a final rub over using ultrafine abrasive to remove any 'woolly' areas prior to applying your finish of choice.

Madrone will accept all surface and penetrative finishes, including dyes, and can be polished to a high lustre if required.

The burr forms are, to my way of thinking, shown off to full effect with a satin or gloss lacquer finish; oil finishes tend to dull the surface somewhat (unlike some other burrs, which are enhanced by oil), and a little of the natural vivacious 'sparkle' is lost. Have a go and see what you think.

Hint

When working wet wood, sand using water as a lubricant to reduce the likelihood of checking and undue darkening of the wood

Vase in madrona burr
by Mark Baker

Gonçalo alves

Astronium fraxinifolium and *A. graveolens*

Other names
Zorrowood,
zebrawood,
tigerwood,
mura

Grows
Brazil, Paraguay and Uruguay
Typical height 120ft (37m)
Trunk diameter 2–3ft (0.6–0.9m)
Specific gravity .95
Typical dry weight 59lb/ft³
(950kg/m³)

Seasoning
Dry the wood slowly to avoid
degrade. There can be a lot of
warping and checking. Rough-turning
and putting it aside to season is a
must when making boxes, bowls or
platters; consider coating the piece
with PVA to retard drying.

**! Possible
health
● risks**
Dermatitis,
irritation to
skin and eyes

Description
The sapwood is up to 4in (100mm) wide,
and grey or brownish-white. The strongly
contrasting heartwood is light golden- to
reddish-brown with irregular streaks or
spots of black and brown. It has a fine,
uniformly textured grain which is irregular
and often interlocked or wavy, alternating
between bands of harder and softer
wood. It is also quite oily. Like many
'exotic' woods, it will darken quickly and
lose its fresh-cut vitality if finishes with UV
inhibitors are not used.

It is available in large sizes, so a wide
variety of decorative, artistic and cabinetry
projects can be undertaken. It is often
used as a substitute for cocobolo
(*Dalbergia retusa*) when highly decorative
pieces are required.

The fine dust from sanding has a
peppery smell that I dislike intensely; it is
also sticky and can be difficult to remove
from clothing.

Working qualities

This is a dense, hard, heavy wood with an oily nature. It cuts well and produces a nice finish off the tool. It does, however, dull cutting edges quickly, including bandsaw blades, so frequent sharpening or replacement will be necessary. Because of the interlocking grain, it may pluck out if you are not very careful when working it. It responds well to a final pass or two with a freshly honed scraper on larger areas to remove any surface ripples; the wood's density makes it difficult to remove these with abrasives.

A bit tricky to sand, it has a tendency to clog the abrasive, and shows every score from the sanding process. It is absolutely necessary to work through the grades, removing all previous scratches before moving on to the next grade of abrasive. It can be prone to heat-checking, so do not work with old, worn-out abrasive and do not use undue pressure; both of these will cause excessive frictional heat. It will polish to a high lustre and accepts all finishes. Because of its density the penetrative finishes such as oils do not penetrate very deeply, but they do polish well.

Hint
Buffing with a powered buffing mop loaded with a micro-abrasive after finishing with oil or a surface finish will produce an exceptionally smooth, tactile surface, excellent for small boxes, hollow forms and bowls

Multi-centred box by Chris Stott

Silver birch

Betula pendula (syn. B. verrucosa) and B. pubescens

Other names
European birch; downy or hairy birch (*B. pubescens*); also English, Finnish, Swedish birch, and additionally according to figure: flame, ice, curly birch

Ripple figure

! Possible health • risks
Dermatitis and respiratory health problems

Grows

Europe, including UK and Scandinavia; grows further north than any other broad-leaved tree

Height 60–70ft (18–21m)
Trunk diameter 2–3ft (0.6–0.9m)
Specific gravity .66
Typical dry weight 41lb/ft³ (660kg/m³)

Seasoning

The wood must be dried rapidly to avoid fungal attacks. It is also slightly prone to warping. Rough-turning followed by further seasoning is a must for larger work, so as to avoid undue movement.

Description

The heartwood and sapwood alike can range from creamy-white to pale brown. The wood is usually straight- and fine-grained with even texture, and has a lustrous appearance and a delicate grain pattern. Irregularities in the grain can cause both flame and curly figuring. Birch is also prone to spalting, which can create dramatic colouring and patterning effects.

This underrated wood has a wonderful silky lustre that turners can exploit to the full. It will mellow to a light tan after a while, but will retain its natural lustre.

Working qualities

This is a hard, tough wood of medium density that cuts well in most instances, provided care is taken with figured pieces. It doesn't always produce nice ribbon-like shavings, but not all woods do. It is available in quite large sizes, so a range of projects can be undertaken, my favourites being platters and hollow forms using figured wood. Plain close-grained timber is suitable for kitchenware. It cuts well with bevel-rubbing tools most of the time, though occasionally it can be a bit woolly – especially when turned wet – and tear-out may occur in the vicinity of cross grain or knots. Shear-scraping can sometimes improve a gouge-cut surface; conventional scraping, even with a delicate touch, may cause the grain to pluck out. For wet-turning, figured wood, which will move erratically as it dries, is best.

Spalted wood can degrade quickly, so a balance must be struck between having enough spalting to make it interesting and allowing it to become too rotten to work with.

Sanding and finishing are no problem. Birch readily accepts all finishes, but can be a little 'hungry', requiring several coats to avoid a blotchy look. Oil is particularly good at enhancing the already warm lustre of the wood. Dyeing is effective, especially on figured pieces.

Hint

When working with spalted wood that is on the soft side, saturate the wood with a 40-50% thinned solution of sanding sealer. Allow it to dry fully, and then turn to a fine finish. The sealer will harden the fibres of the wood enough to allow you to turn them without too much pluck-out

Box in spalted birch by Mark Baker

Boxwood

Buxus sempervirens

Other names
Box; often identified also by country of origin, e.g. Iranian box

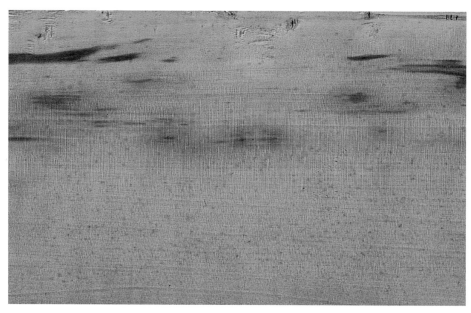

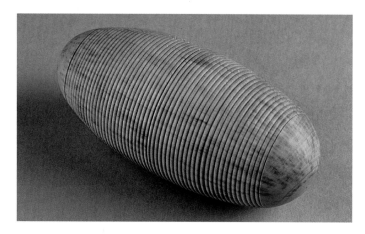

Spalted figure
(box by Mark Baker)

Possible health risks
Dermatitis; dust is an irritant to eyes, nose and throat

Grows
UK, mainland Europe, Turkey, western Asia

Height 20–30ft (6–9m)

Trunk diameter up to 8in (0.2m), but usually less than 6in (150mm)

Specific gravity .91

Typical dry weight 57lb/ft^3 (910kg/m^3)

Seasoning
Owing to its small diameter, box is mainly dried in the round. End-coating is essential to minimize splitting, but in truth, even with very slow air-drying under cover, it is very common to experience splitting along the length of the piece, rendering the wood unusable except for small items. It may be necessary to rough-turn the wood to stabilize it prior to finish-turning, especially when making boxes with close-fitting lids. For other types of project you might consider using partially seasoned timber, bearing in mind that it will move a little.

Description

Varying in colour from butter to lemon yellow, boxwood is dense, hard and heavy. It has a beautiful, fine, uniform texture, and the heart and sapwood are not clearly differentiated. Tight, pippy knots and fungal staining are fairly common. It is usually straight-grained but can occasionally be irregular. Only available in small pieces, it is commonly used for boxes, small hollow forms, and bowls. Its ability to hold very fine detail without breaking out means that it is also prized for small carved work, and it is one of the few woods that are suitable for hand-chased screw threads.

Working qualities

This is a fantastic timber to work with – one of the nicest you are likely to encounter. It's just a shame that it's not available in larger sizes. What it lacks in size it more than makes up for in its ability to hold very fine detail, and the ease with which it can be turned. It cuts well with all tools: even with a conventional scraper, long ribbon shavings can be produced, leaving a surface that may not require sanding. If it does, it will only be necessary to use fine grades. This is a wood that can be wet-turned to good effect; an even, thin wall thickness is necessary to reduce the risk of splitting.

Box responds well to sanding; wet-sanding will reduce the frictional heat and the risk of heat-checking. When the wood is dry, it accepts all finishes. As with most woods, residual moisture can cause some surface finishes to flake off because they cannot properly bond into the fibres.

For thread-chasing, be sure to use clean, stain-free wood. Fungal infection or spalting can make the wood a little softer than normal and cause the chased threads to break out. The end grain will also hold a chatter pattern well.

Hint
When chasing threads, a little paste wax will act as a lubricant, making cutting easier still

Natural-edged box in spalted boxwood by Chris Stott

Sweet chestnut

Castanea sativa

Other names
European chestnut, Spanish chestnut

Figured sample

Grows
Europe, chiefly south-west and Mediterranean areas
Height 100–115ft (30–50m)
Trunk diameter 5ft (1.5m)
Specific gravity .54
Typical dry weight 34lb/ft³ (540kg/m³)

Seasoning
This wood is difficult to dry. It is best dried slowly, and is liable to degrade, suffering from cell collapse and honeycombing. The movement in service is small. Where accuracty is required, rough-turning is a must, to stabilize the wood prior to finish-turning. Alternatively, wet-turn it to completion and then allow the piece to move.

Description

A delightful wood whose heartwood is light brown to yellow-brown; not dissimilar to oak in appearance, but with finer or less prominent rays on quartersawn surfaces. The sapwood is very thin and pale, and distinct from the heartwood. The grain is usually straight but it is not unusual to see spiral grain in older trees. (Spiral growth is often visible on the outside of the trunk also.) The colouring is distinctive and very beautiful; it sometimes has darker brown streaks running through it. The texture is coarse, and shakes can frequently be found in older trees. Although chestnut rarely forms burrs (burls), figuring is not uncommon, and adds a further dimension to this wonderful timber.

Available in large sizes, chestnut is suitable for many projects. It is often used in the cabinetmaking trade as a substitute for oak. Other common uses include artistic and ornamental turning, domestic ware and furniture parts.

Working qualities

Though chestnut resembles oak, it is easier to work. It is a medium-density wood and, when newly seasoned, cuts cleanly with freshly sharpened tools. Shear-scraping will produce a finer finish than conventional scraping, but by far the best finish comes from bevel-rubbing tools. The wood has a sweet smell when freshly cut. Because of the tannic acid in it, it may stain hands and steel blue. If left in contact with steel too long it can corrode it, causing surface pitting, so clean the lathe and tools well after using it.

It sands well with either wet or dry sanding methods, and finishes well, but if you require an absolutely smooth surface finish you will need to fill the grain. Either apply many coats of a surface lacquer, cutting back between coats to fill the open grain (this is my preferred option), or treat with a grain filler before applying the finish of your choice.

This is another underrated wood that I recommend you try.

Platter by Mark Baker, finished with oil

Cedar of Lebanon
Cedrus libani

Other names
True cedar

Ripple figure
around a knot

**Possible
health
risks**
Respiratory
problems,
rhinitis

Grows
Middle east, UK, USA
Height 80ft (24m)
Trunk diameter 3ft (0.9m)
Specific gravity .56
Typical dry weight 35lb/ft³
(560kg/m³)

Seasoning
There is a slight tendency to warp,
but the wood dries easily with little
degrade. Highly figured areas can
move a lot in seasoning. The wood
can be turned wet or partially
seasoned, but will move. Kiln-dried
stock is fine for most uses, but for
accurate work rough-turning is best.

Description

Most hobby turners focus mainly on hardwoods, but cedar of Lebanon is one of many beautiful softwoods which are well worth exploring. (Others include yew (*Taxus baccata*), redwood (*Sequoia sempervirens*) and thuya (*Tetraclinis articulata*). The heartwood ranges from a light toffee brown to greenish-orange or yellow. The latewood is clearly distinct, being darker and denser than the pale-coloured earlywood. The sapwood is thin, and whitish or yellow-grey in colour. This soft, light timber has a medium to fine texture, and the grain is normally straight, with a clearly defined pattern. Bark inclusions and large knots are often found, and the outer edges of the annual rings can be rippled or wavy. The wood is resinous and has a strong scent, similar to a sweet incense. Large sizes are available, giving a lot of scope for various projects. It is used in joinery, cabinetmaking and decorative and artistic turnery. Note that many other, unrelated woods are also marketed as 'cedar'.

Working qualities

Cedar of Lebanon cuts well with bevel-rubbing tools and does not blunt tool edges very quickly. The wood will come off the tool in ribbons, except when working old wood, which has a tendency to be dusty. End grain or cross grain around knots may tend to pull out if you use scrapers in conventional mode; shear-scraping is a better option, but gouges and skew chisels are better still.

Cedar of Lebanon sands and finishes well, and accepts both surface and penetrative finishes. It will polish to a wonderful sheen, which gives the wood a silky look and feel. The knots can be very hard and resinous, so care is needed to avoid sanding hollows around the harder areas, and there is a very real chance of clogging when sanding the knots. There is often swirling grain around the knots, which is not a problem to cut, but may form stunning patterns and figure which turners can exploit to the fullest. The downside is that shakes or splits may occur in these areas.

Hint

If you wet-sand the cedar, any splits or shakes will be filled with the sanding slurry. This slurry sets in the wood as the oil oxidizes and dries. It is not a perfect blend, but better than a shop-bought filler

Bowl by Mark Baker, finished with oil

Putumuju

Centrolobium spp.

Other names
Canarywood,
araribá,
porcupinewood

Oil finish

Grows
Southern Brazil, Ecuador, Panama
Height 100ft (30m)
Trunk diameter 2ft 6in–4ft
(0.75–1.2m)
Specific gravity 0.75–1.00
according to species
Typical dry weight 47–62lb/ft³
(750–1000kg/m³)

Seasoning
Putumuju dries at a moderate rate and does not usually warp or suffer from splitting or checking. Shrinkage is minimal. It can be turned wet to completion, but if you are making boxes or other work where accuracy of shape is required, rough-turning and setting it aside to dry is recommended. On some of the more figured pieces it may be necessary to even out the drying process by coating the rough-turned blank with PVA before setting it aside to season further.

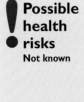

**Possible
health
risks**
Not known

Description

This is a lovely wood to look at. The heartwood is variegated yellow to orange, and sometimes tinged with a rainbow of colours. Sadly, it changes quickly to a mid orange-brown with some variegated stripes. The sapwood is yellow and clearly distinct from the heartwood. The grain may be straight or irregular. It is quite fine-grained, will hold fine detail, and can be carved with hand or power tools.

Although the trunk is a medium size, it is difficult to get even moderately large sections. Usually one is restricted to buying pre-dimensioned blanks of a fairly small size, suitable for decorative or artistic work.

Working qualities

This is a lovely wood to turn, wet or seasoned – if only all woods were this easy to work. Its only real shortcoming is that it is not available in larger sizes. It cuts well with all tools, but the best finish is obtained from bevel-rubbing tools. Scrapers give good results, especially when shear-scraping, but a little more sanding will be needed.

It sands well, but watch out for heat-checking on end grain. It can be finished to a high polish with either surface or penetrative finishes.

Box by Chris Stott

Hint

I find that oils diminish the look of this wood. My favourite finish is sanding sealer, followed by a coat of paste wax which has UV inhibitors in it. This combination seems not to darken the natural colour of the wood too much, and helps to maintain that fresh look for some time

Ziracote

Cordia dodecandra

Other names
Ziricote,
zircote,
sericote,
siricote,
canalete,
peterebi,
laurel

Grows
Belize, Guatemala, Mexico
Height 60–90ft (20–28m)
Trunk diameter 2ft 6in (0.75m)
max.
Specific gravity .65–.85
Typical dry weight 41–53lb/ft³
(650–850kg/m³)

Seasoning
The wood is slow-drying and fairly
difficult to season. It is prone to
surface checking and may develop
end splits. Rough-turning and then
setting it aside to season further is
recommended. Coating the whole
piece or just the end grain in PVA
will even out the drying process and
reduce the likelihood of checking
or splitting.

 **Possible
health
risks**
Not known

Description
The brownish-yellow sapwood is clearly
distinguished from the heartwood. The
latter is a reddish-brown colour with
irregular wavy, dark streaks. Dark
markings on the wood often run at an
angle to the main axis of the tree, making
a pattern which is unique and highly
decorative. The erratic nature of these
markings means that you are never quite
sure what the piece will be like until you
start to cut it; the result can be a real
treat. It usually has straight or interlocked
grain, a fine to medium texture and an
average lustre. It is a medium-density
timber that holds fine detail well. Not
often found in large sizes, it is mainly
used for artistic and decorative turning.

Working qualities

Ziracote cuts well with gouges and scrapers, but you will need to sharpen the tools regularly. It will, more often than not, produce chips and dust rather than ribbon shavings; this is a result of the interlocking grain, and does not indicate that the grain is pulling out. Ziracote blunts bandsaw blades quickly. Chatterwork is possible on the end grain, but the wood is not hard enough to hold a hand-chased thread. It can be carved, preferably with power tools. It is suitable for wet-turning to completion, and produces little dust when turned wet.

Dry rather than wet sanding is recommended to avoid colour contamination. But be careful: seasoned wood produces a lot of acrid, choking dust when turned or sanded, and it is prone to heat-checking. Use fresh abrasive when sanding, and work through the grades. The wood can be brought to a very fine finish.

This is a beautiful wood whose colour pigmentation is always throwing up surprises. Some woods come alive in large-scale work, but I think ziracote is a real gem when used to create well-crafted, delicate, small pieces.

Hint
Chatterwork on end grain is difficult to clean up once created. Use sharp tools to start with, to make sure that you get a clean cut that will only require polishing

Bowl by Bert Marsh

Brazilian tulipwood

Dalbergia frutescens and related species

Other names
Pau rosa,
bois de rose,
pinkwood,
pau de fuso,
jacarandá rosa.
Not to be
confused with
American
tulipwood
(*Liriodendron
tulipifera*), which
is not related

Grows
Mainly north-east Brazil, Columbia,
Guyana and Venezuela
Height and diameter As the tree
is small and the trunk irregular in
shape, it is generally sold in small
billets
Specific gravity .96
Typical dry weight 60lb/ft³
(960kg/m³)

Seasoning
This wood usually dries without any
problems, with a low risk of twisting
and checking.
    To avoid movement, rough-turning
and setting it aside to season further
is recommended. Alternatively, the
wood can be turned to completion
wet or partially seasoned, but will
distort a bit.

**Possible
health
risks**
Not known

Description

A wood that shouts it presence far and
wide, Brazilian tulipwood is dense, hard
and heavy, with an oily feel to it. The very
distinctive creamy-yellow sapwood
contrasts well with the heartwood, which
has a variegated striped figure in various
shades of soft pink, rose, violet or maroon
on a cream or straw-coloured
background. This really is one of the
peacocks of the wood world. After
exposure to light, the fantastic colouring
will mellow down a little, the rich markings
remaining distinct but losing a little of their
fresh-cut vibrancy. The grain can vary from
straight to roey and can be erratic,
irregular and interlocking. The wood is fine
in texture and has a natural high lustre.
    The small sizes available may be
thought to restrict its possible uses, but
if this vibrant wood were available in
sufficient size for a platter, imagine how
gaudy it would be! Smaller is definitely
better, to maximize the impact of this
stunning wood.

Working qualities

Tulipwood can be a little tricky to work: although close-grained and dense, it is liable to splinter a little. This problem is most common when using it for furniture-making, but it can occasionally happen when turning. Sharp tools and a considered, careful cut will help no end. Having said that, for the most part this is a well-behaved wood and a pleasure to work. It yields a fine finish straight from the tool, which may require only minimal sanding to remove minor blemishes.

It can be subject to heat-checking, so care is needed when sanding. It wet-sands well, provided no sapwood is present to cause colour contamination. Dry sanding will produce a lot of very fine dust that has a peppery smell. Although there is no data available to suggest that this wood has definite health risks associated with it, remember that all dust is potentially harmful, and take adequate precautions against inhaling it. The wood can be finished to a high polish with both penetrative and surface finishes.

Hint
A lacquer spray finish with UV inhibitor will help maintain the fresh-cut vibrancy of the colour

Bowl by Bert Marsh

Sonokeling rosewood

Dalbergia latifolia

Other names
Indian rosewood, East Indian rosewood, Bombay blackwood, Indian palisander, Java palisander, malabar, shisham, biti, eravidi, kalaruk

Box by Chris Stott

! Possible health risks
Dermatitis, asthma and respiratory problems

Grows
India
Height 100ft (30m)
Trunk diameter 2ft 6in (0.75m), sometimes broader
Specific gravity .85
Typical dry weight 53lb/ft³ (850kg/m³)

Seasoning
The wood dries quite quickly with very little degrade. However, let it dry too quickly and end-splitting and surface checking may occur. It responds well to rough-turning and setting it aside to stabilize and dry further. Turners often use this timber in small sizes for making boxes with close-fitting lids, in which case it is essential to stabilize it by rough-turning so as to maintain the fit. It is suitable for wet turning, if you can get large enough pieces.

Description

This beautiful wood is hard, dense and heavy. The heartwood varies from rich rose to a deep brown with dark purple-black lines streaking through it, resulting in a very attractive pattern. It has a narrow, interlocking, cross grain with a moderately coarse and uniform texture. When quartersawn, it can display a wonderful ribbon figure. The sapwood, which is distinct from the heartwood, has a yellowish-white tinge, sometimes with a hint of purple colouring. Fresh-cut wood has a pleasant smell, but this wears off as it dries. The name 'sonokeling' is used for wood which is plantation-grown. When finished well this is a beautiful-looking wood. It is used extensively in the furniture trade, for high-class joinery and for artistic and decorative turnings.

Working qualities

This hard, dense wood frequently contains mineral deposits that will blunt bandsaw blades and other cutting edges quickly, sometimes severely. That said, it turns satisfactorily with most tools. The best cuts are with bevel-rubbing tools, but frequent sharpening may be necessary to maintain an effective edge. Having a moderately course texture, it does not, in my experience, hold very fine detail without breaking out.

The wood will darken with age, mellowing to a rich, deep brown that will continue to show the dark streaks running through it.

It usually sands well, especially with the wet sanding method, but heat-checking may occur if excessive heat is generated. The grain may need filling if a super-smooth surface is required; however, wet sanding causes the grain to fill with the sanding slurry, and this should be sufficient. Dry sanding will result in a lot of irritant dust being produced, so either use efficient dust extraction, or wet-sand. Sonokeling is receptive to both surface and penetrative finishes.

Hint

There can be a bit of break-out towards the edges of the work, so be careful and take the finishing cuts with very sharp tools

Box by John Hunnex

African blackwood
Dalbergia melanoxylon

Other names
Mozambique ebony, mpingo, African grenadillo, pau preto

Grows
Eastern Africa
Height 15–20ft (4.5–6m)
Trunk diameter Rarely more than 1ft (0.3m)
Specific gravity 1.2
Typical dry weight 75lb/ft³ (1200kg/m³)

Seasoning
This is a very slow-drying wood and it can take 2–3 years to be fully seasoned. It is part-seasoned in log or billet form, then converted, end-coated and stacked under cover. Problems with heart shakes and end splitting mean that only small sections are commonly available. Rough-turning and setting the pieces aside for further drying is recommended.

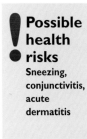
Possible health risks
Sneezing, conjunctivitis, acute dermatitis

Description
This very dense, dark, oily wood is sometimes referred to as an ebony, but in fact it is related to the rosewoods. (The real ebonies are *Diospyros* spp.) The sapwood is narrow and a soft yellow-cream in colour, providing a stark contrast to the heartwood which is a dark, rich purple-brown with black streaks. The grain is often straight, but can vary. It is one of the blackest, darkest, densest timbers a turner is likely to encounter. Most people assume it is solid black, but if you look closely you will see that there is a delicate but distinct grain pattern. The wood can be slightly oily to the touch, and is very fine and even-textured, heavy and hard. It is only available in small sizes, which limits the turning possibilities, but its looks are stunning, especially when heartwood and sapwood are contrasted. It is used for woodwind instruments, decorative or artistic turning, and cabinetmaking.

Working qualities

This is a wonderful wood to work with. Being dense and very fine-grained, it will hold very fine detail and is probably the best wood to use for thread-chasing by hand. The wood cuts well but blunts tools quickly, and has a severe blunting effect on bandsaw blades. Long ribbon shavings are rare; instead, you are likely to get small curls, sometimes chips, and invariably quite a lot of dust. The dust is a pain, but the end results are worthwhile. Try turning a natural-edge piece incorporating some sapwood: the vivid contrast with the heartwood gives a stunning effect.

Blackwood is often used with other woods, to provide a contrasting accent. White or cream woods such as holly (*Ilex* spp.) or boxwood (*Buxus sempervirens*), and red or orange woods like padauk (*Pterocarpus* spp.), work particularly well.

It is prone to heat-checking, so care is needed when sanding. If no sapwood is present it can be wet-sanded. Dry sanding will produce a lot of noxious dust. Finishing is easy and the wood can be taken to a high lustre. Minute checks can be filled with cyanoacrylate adhesive and sanded while the adhesive is still wet; the mixture of dust and adhesive will set and fill the crack.

Hint

I think a satin to high-gloss finish is needed to bring out the beauty of this wood to the fullest. Power buffing will greatly help to achieve a lustrous finish

Bowl by Bert Marsh

Cocobolo

Dalbergia retusa

Other names
Granadillo,
Nicaraguan
rosewood,
pau preto,
caviuna, nambar,
cocobolo
prieto,
palo negro,
palo sandro

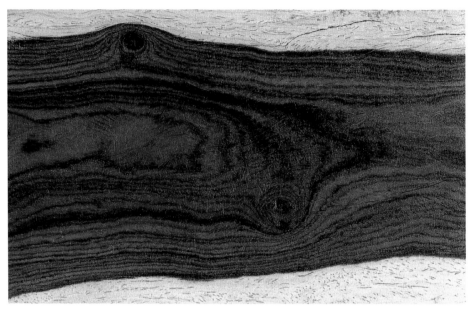

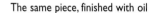
The same piece, finished with oil

Grows
Pacific areas of Central America
Height 45–60ft (13–18m)
Trunk diameter 1ft 6in–2ft
(0.5–0.6m)
Specific gravity 1.10
Typical dry weight 68lb/ft³
(1100kg/m³)

! ● Possible health risks
**Skin irritation
from dust;
dermatitis,
conjunctivitis,
nausea,
bronchial
asthma and
irritation to
the nose and
throat**

Box by Chris Stott in cocobolo burr (burl)

Seasoning
It dries very slowly, with a tendency
to split and check, and should be air-
dried rather than kilned. The wood is
stable in use, as the natural oil
content acts as a barrier to water
absorption. However, rough-turning
and setting it aside to season further
is essential to prevent undue
movement if you are making fine or
delicate items such as boxes.

Description

This rosewood species is another one that draws attention to itself: both visually and physically it is a beautiful wood. Cocobolo is a close-grained wood and will hold fine detail. When it is newly cut, the heartwood shows many colours, including rich, deep reds with orange and yellow streaks. When the wood is exposed to air it can darken to a deep red or orange-red with black and purple streaks. It is very hard, dense and heavy, with an oily feel. Usually the grain is straight, although it can sometimes be interlocking, irregular and variable. More often than not it has a fine, even texture. The clear sapwood is a creamy-white colour which contrasts well with the heartwood.

Cocobolo will lose a lot of its fresh-cut vibrancy on exposure to light. The wood will darken considerably over time, taking on a much richer brown colouring; the streaks remain visible. It is available in reasonable sizes, but more often than not it is used to make highly decorative small pieces, where the beauty of the grain pattern is shown to its fullest.

Working qualities

This is a wood that cuts well on the lathe, producing small curled shavings rather than long ribbons from the gouge. It can create quite a bit of fine dust, which is oily, clings to surfaces, and will also stain clothing. The finish from the cut can be exceptionally good. It cuts well with scrapers, but best with gouges and skews. If the oily dust sticks to the bevel of the tool, it needs to be cleared from time to time to ensure a controlled cut. The wood can be used for chasing threads by hand, although it is not as good as boxwood (*Buxus sempervirens*) or African blackwood (*Dalbergia melanoxylon*). It will hold very fine detail and is suitable for carving.

Cocobolo is prone to heat-checking, so sanding should be undertaken with care, working through the grades with fresh, sharp abrasive and a light touch. As long as sapwood is not present, it can be wet-sanded; this will avoid the fine, choking dust that is produced by dry sanding. Because of its oily nature, some surface finishes (lacquer, for example) may occasionally fail to adhere firmly; it can also gum up bandsaw blades a little. Adhesion can also be a problem when trying to glue cocobolo. There is no difficulty in using oil as a finish.

Hint

If applying a surface finish such as lacquer, wipe the work over first with a cellulose thinner to clean the surface and remove any oiliness

Bowl by John Hunnex

Macassar ebony

Diospyros celebica

Other names
Coromandel, calamander wood, camagon, Indian ebony, tendu, temru, timbruni, tunki. *D. tomentosa*, *D. marmorata*, *D. melanoxylon* and *D. ebenum* are related species with slightly different characteristics

Grows
South India, Sri Lanka, Philippines, Indonesia
Height 50ft (15m)
Trunk diameter 1ft–1ft 6in (0.3–0.45m)
Specific gravity 1.09
Typical dry weight 68lb/ft³ (1090kg/m³)

Seasoning
The wood should be seasoned slowly, and the trees are sometimes girdled for two years prior to felling. Deep, long checks or hairline shakes can develop, and fast drying will result in end-splits and surface checking. It is advisable to rough-turn the pieces and leave them to dry further before use, if accuracy and stability are required.

Possible health risks
Dust can cause sneezing, acute dermatitis and conjunctivitis

Description
Macassar ebony is a strikingly beautiful wood which is very heavy, very dense and very hard. It is close-grained, and the grain is usually straight but can occasionally be wavy or irregular. The wood has a fine, even texture with a metallic sheen. The heartwood is black or sometimes grey, with streaks running through it which range from light biscuit through light brown or reddish-brown to deep brown. The colour range of the streaking is a real treat, giving a lot of variety to the wood. The sapwood contrasts well with the heartwood and is a creamy biscuit-brown colour.

This wood is proof positive that ebonies are not solid black. There is rich colour variation in all the ebonies – sometimes subtle, but always surprising.

Working qualities

Macassar ebony is a very brittle wood that can be difficult to work: the grain is liable to tear out and the edges may splinter off. It blunts cutting edges quickly, including bandsaw blades, and tends to produce a lot of dust. That said, it is a wood worth persevering with if you are looking for the 'wow factor'. With sharp tools and a gentle cut the grain tear-out should be minimal, but great care needs to be taken when using a scraper. Honing will help to some extent, but the finish from the scraper is still unlikely to be as good as you can get from a gouge. Shear-scraping will improve things a little, but to be honest you are better off trying to get as good a finish as you can off the gouge and then sanding to remove any small surface defects.

Sand carefully to avoid heat-checking; do not wet-sand, or you might contaminate the contrasting colours. However, dry sanding will produce a lot of fine dust; this carries known health risks, so make sure you extract it effectively and do not have prolonged exposure to it. Work through the grades of abrasive, and finish with the product of your choice. The surface can be taken to a high gloss, but the beautiful patterning is, in my opinion, shown to best effect with a satin sheen.

Bowl by John Hunnex

Hint
Any minute splits or checks can be filled either with coloured wax, or with cyanoacrylate adhesive which is sanded whilst still wet so that it is tinted by the sanding dust – but you will have to work quickly

River red gum

Eucalyptus camaldulensis, syn. E. rostrata

Other names
Red river gum,
Murray red
gum, red gum,
river gum,
Queensland
blue gum

Burr (burl)

**Possible
health
risks**
Not known

Grows
Australia
Height 65ft (20m) but can reach up
to 115ft (35m)
Trunk diameter 6ft (2m)
Specific gravity .82
Typical dry weight 51lb/ft³
(825kg/m³)

Seasoning
This wood dries well, provided much
care is taken, but there are
sometimes problems with
longitudinal shrinkage and distortion
caused by gum pockets. It can be
turned wet or partially seasoned, but
may move a lot, and the movement
is unpredictable. If stabilized wood is
required, then rough-turning followed
by further drying will help. When
rough-turning highly figured pieces,
allow an extra ¼–½in (6–13mm) of
wall thickness per 12in (300mm)
overall diameter.

Description

The heartwood can range from vibrant pink through soft red or orange to a reddish-brown, and is distinct from the paler sapwood. The grain is interlocked and often wavy, with a pleasant pattern to it. When quartersawn, a fiddleback or mottled figure can be present. This wood is of medium density and has a fine, even texture, but veins of gum can be present. It mellows quickly to a mid-brown colour unless a finish with a UV inhibitor is used. It can form burrs, which vary in figure from tight clusters of knots to, more commonly, swirling grain. This delightful wood is available in quite large sizes, so it has many possible uses.

Working qualities

This medium-dense wood is capable of holding quite reasonable fine detail. It is a wood that cuts well with gouges, producing ribbon shavings when freshly seasoned. The gum pockets and interlocking grain that may occur do not normally present a problem to the turner who works with sharp tools and takes delicate finishing cuts, but some pluck-out from the interlocking grain may occur when scraping, so shear-scraping is recommended to achieve a smoother finish.

Wet turning is most effective when there is some figure in the wood. This will create differential shrinkage rates that may cause the wood to move and distort more.

There are no problems with either sanding or finishing. Wet sanding is a possibility with this wood, but if there are many gum pockets the oily slurry will be forced into these and may look odd if not cleaned out. A high polish can be achieved if required. I recommend an oil finish to create a warm, rich glow that shows up the grain wonderfully.

Hint

When the wood has been wet-turned, wet-sand using water as a lubricant and allow to dry fully; then rub over with a very fine grade of abrasive (600–800 grit) prior to applying the final finish of your choice

Bowl by John Hunnex

Tasmanian oak

Eucalyptus delegatensis, E. obliqua and E. regnans

Other names
Alpine ash,
white-top or
gum-top
stringybark,
woollybutt
(*E. delegatensis*);
messmate
stringybark,
brown-top
stringybark
(*E. obliqua*);
stringy gum,
swamp gum,
Victorian ash
(*E. regnans*). All
three species
are sold as
'Tasmanian oak'

Ripple figure

Grows
South-east Australia and Tasmania
Height 200–300ft (60–90m)
Trunk diameter 3–7ft (1–2.3m)
Specific gravity .62–.78
Typical dry weight 39–49lb/ft³
(620–780kg/m³)

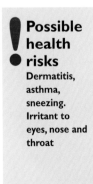
**Possible
health
risks**
Dermatitis,
asthma,
sneezing.
Irritant to
eyes, nose and
throat

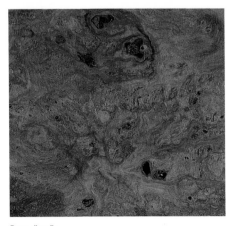
Burr (burl)

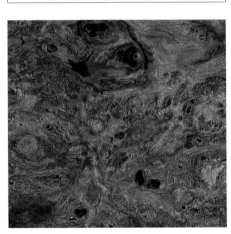
Burr with oiled finish

Seasoning

This wood dries quite rapidly, but if care is not taken there is a high risk of distortion, surface checking, internal checking and collapse. As the wood moves quite a lot it is an ideal candidate for wet turning; but if stable timber is needed, rough-turn your piece, leaving an extra ¼in (6mm) or more of wall thickness for every 12in (300mm) diameter to allow for the increased level of warping and distortion which is likely with this wood, and set it aside to dry further before turning to completion. You may like to coat the end grain of the rough-turned piece with PVA glue to even out the drying rate.

Working qualities

Tasmanian oak is a nice wood to work with. It does tend to blunt tool edges a little, especially bandsaw blades, but does not present the turner with any major problems. As with any wood, sharp tools are required to achieve a clean cut. Conventional scraping may pluck up the grain a little; shear-scraping is a more delicate approach and will help to remove any defects. If this doesn't work, make a new, delicate cut with a gouge, followed by a gentle finishing cut, then sand. The wood can be wet-turned to completion. It also carves well with hand tools, but better still with power tools.

Sanding and finishing are not a problem. This wood can be wet-sanded to achieve a very fine surface prior to applying the finish of your choice. It can also be taken to a very high polish if required.

Hint

Tasmanian oak stains well, and staining can be used to enhance the grain when figuring is present

Bowl by Bert Marsh

Description

A medium-dense wood that has a slight blunting effect on tools. The heartwood is usually a pale creamy-tan to pale brown colour with a pinkish tinge. The sapwood is paler and not distinct from the heartwood. The grain is usually straight but can be wavy or interlocked. It has a coarse, open, even texture and the growth rings are often clearly visible. The wood is neither a true ash nor a true oak; it resembles plainsawn European oak (*Quercus robur* or *Q. petraea*), but without the silver grain. It produces delightful burrs and, as with many woods, there is a lot of colour variation from piece to piece – especially in the burrs, which can range from a rich orange-tan to a soft brown. Sometimes gum veins are present. It mellows quickly on exposure to light, and loses its fresh-cut look. Available in quite large sizes, it can be used for a variety of projects.

Jarrah

Eucalyptus marginata

Other names
None

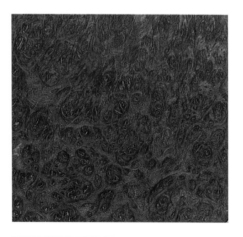

Burr (burl)
with oil finish

Seasoning

Jarrah needs careful drying, and it is best to air-dry before kiln-drying. Wide stock may check or warp whilst drying, and collapse can often occur. To minimize movement, rough-turning to allow the wood to stabilize and dry is recommended. This is also a great wood to use if you want to turn your work wet and then let it move as it wants. Wet-turned burrs will dry to create a nice 'hammered' effect across the surface, which is very pleasing to look at and to touch.

Grows

South-west Australia
Height 100–150ft (30–45m)
Trunk diameter 3–6ft (0.9–1.8m)
Specific gravity .80
Typical dry weight 50lb/ft³
(800kg/m³)

! **Possible health risks**
Irritation to eyes, nose and throat

Description

This is a medium-dense, hard, heavy wood whose heartwood varies from pink through rich orange-red to brownish-red. It is sometimes marked by short, dark flecks on the end grain, with crescent-shaped flecks on the flatsawn surface. It often has dark brown or black streaks, and sometimes has bark inclusions. The colour is variable, and can change to a rich mahogany-red on exposure to light. Over time, the wood darkens considerably with exposure. The grain is usually straight but can be interlocked or wavy, and it has a moderately coarse, even texture. Veins and gum pockets are commonly found. The sapwood is a creamy-yellow colour and is distinct from the heartwood, but darkens with age. It often forms burrs, and both burrs and trunk wood are available in nice large dimensions, enabling a wide range of projects to be undertaken. The burr form is a stunning wood to work with.

Working qualities

Jarrah is a gorgeous wood to work with, especially the burrs. It can be a little tricky to turn, however. Seasoned timber does not produce long ribbon shavings; instead it usually makes short, curly shavings or chippings, all of which are accompanied by a dirty dust. This applies to both the burr and the standard form of the wood. The interlocking grain and the figured areas with irregular grain are prone to plucking out, and the edges of the work may be brittle and inclined to splinter. Scraping tools used in the conventional mode will often pluck the grain, so I find it best to work with gouges and then delicately scrape to refine the surface, accepting that there is a possibility of tear-out. With light cuts this will not amount to very much, and can be dealt with by sanding afterwards.

Jarrah can be sanded wet or dry. With burr wood, wet sanding may result in the open structure filling with sanding slurry, which can be unsightly and may need to be cleaned out before applying finish. Because the wood may have gum pockets, especially in burrs, oil is my favoured form of finish for jarrah. After oiling, I power-buff the work to form a deep satin sheen that really enhances the beautiful features of this wonderful wood. That said, good results can be achieved with either surface or penetrative finishes.

Hint

If you are going to use oil as a finish, give the work a preliminary coat of oil once the initial profiling is complete, and let this soak in before making the final cuts with a gouge or scraper. This will give a finer finish from the cut

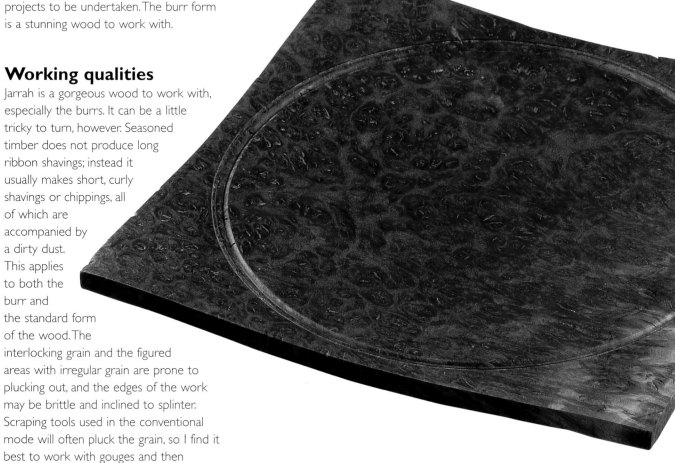

Platter by Mark Baker

European beech
Fagus sylvatica

Other names
English, Danish, French, Romanian beech, depending on country of origin

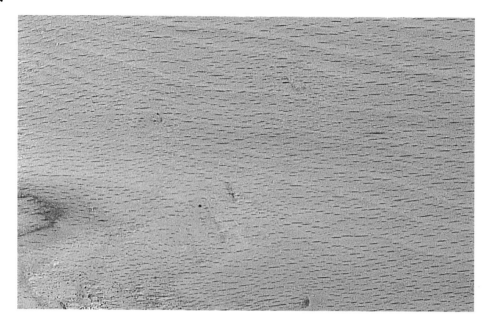

Box by Mark Baker in beech burr (burl)

Possible health risks
Dermatitis, eye irritation, decrease in lung function, rare incidence of nasal cancer

Grows
Throughout central Europe and Britain; also western Asia
Height 100ft (30m)
Trunk diameter 4ft (1.2m)
Specific gravity .72
Typical dry weight 45lb/ft³ (720kg/m³)

Seasoning
The wood dries fairly rapidly but may warp, check and shrink, so care is needed whether air- or kiln-drying. Spindle work for furniture and joinery can be made from well-seasoned air-dried beech which has been stored in a heated workshop, or from kiln-dried stock of about 10–12% moisture content; but for items such as hollow forms, boxes or bowls, rough-turning followed by further seasoning is advisable.

Description

Beech is a moderately dense wood whose heartwood is very similar in colour to the sapwood. The colour of both can vary from a creamy white to a very pale tan; it may even darken to a pale pink or a pale brown. Steaming may produce a pinkish red. Sometimes the wood has a dark red heart, or darker veining. It has a straight grain with a fine, even texture, and a characteristic fleck. When quartersawn, it may exhibit an attractive broad ray figure on radial surfaces. It can hold quite fine detail.

Beech is a wood that will regularly spalt, given the right conditions. The amount of spalting varies considerably from piece to piece, and can result in an exquisite marble-like appearance. Spalted beech is often used to produce dramatic artistic pieces such as hollow forms and boxes, but it can be somewhat soft. Beech also occasionally forms burrs, which can vary in colour from the parent wood; I have some beech burr that is pink.

This a good timber for wet turning. It is commonly used in the woodworking and furniture industries to create many things from tables and chairs through to architectural items. Turners use beech a great deal, but the spalted wood is most in demand for artistic or decorative items.

Working qualities

Non-spalted beech is ideal for kitchenware and utilitarian work in general, and for turning furniture parts. It is easy to turn, cutting well with all tools, though bevel-rubbing tools give the best results. The spalted timber is highly prized and used extensively on 'artistic' turned work. Spalted wood can be soft, so care is needed when cutting and sanding; soft patches may need 'hardening' to enable proper finishing cuts to be made. Coating the whole piece with shellac or cellulose-based sanding sealer, and then letting it dry, should harden the surface sufficiently to allow a reasonable cut without excessive grain tear-out.

Spalted wood should be sanded dry so as not to contaminate the lighter wood with the fungal spores. Even with dry-sanding, the grey colour from the spores may spread a little, but wet sanding would make this worse. Non-spalted wood can be wet-sanded. There is anecdotal evidence to suggest that the fungal spores in spalted wood may present a health hazard if breathed in, so be careful to minimize exposure and take effective measures to control the dust.

Whether spalted or not, beech sands well and finishes well. Penetrative and surface finishes can be used to good effect.

Hint
Don't use cyanoacrylate adhesive to 'spot'-seal soft wood. The resulting spot coating will remain visible and distinct from the main body colour of the piece

Hollow form in spalted beech by Mark Baker

European ash

Fraxinus excelsior

Other names
Usually distinguished by country of origin

Olive figure
(box by Chris Stott)

Grows
Europe, North Africa, western Asia
Height 80–120ft (25–35m)
Trunk diameter 2–5ft (0.6–1.5m)
Specific gravity .71
Typical dry weight 44lb/ft³
(710kg/m³)

! Possible health • risks
Decrease in lung function, rhinitis, asthma

Ripple figure (hollow form by Mark Baker)

Seasoning

This wood dries fairly quickly but care is needed to avoid splitting and checking. The figured parts, especially the crotch area, are particularly prone to splitting, so rough-turning followed by further seasoning is recommended for artistic work.

Description

Ash is a fantastic wood to work with. It is tough, heavy, straight-grained, flexible, and coarse but even in texture, but does not hold fine detail without breaking out. The grain pattern is very distinctive. Available in large sizes, it is a great wood for utilitarian items such as platters and bowls, as well as 'artistic' turning. It is often used for handles and for architectural work such as balusters and spindles, but this belies the full quality, beauty and versatility of this wood. This is a nice timber for wet turning, where the piece is brought to a thin, even wall thickness and then allowed to distort as it dries.

The sapwood is not easily differentiated from the heartwood. Both are usually a creamy to light tan colour. Sometimes it has a mid- to dark brown or black-streaked heartwood, which resembles olivewood (*Olea europaea*) and is therefore referred to as **olive ash**; this is *not* caused by rot, and can be denser than the standard form. Rippling can also occur quite frequently, but burrs are not so common. A lot of figuring can occur around branches, and the figuring found near the crotch of the tree is fantastic, as with most woods. Ash is available in large sizes, which gives the turner a lot of scope to experiment and play. The wood mellows quickly from its fresh-cut whitish-cream to a tan colour.

Working qualities

Ash is a great wood to work with, wet or dry – thuogh wet wood can produce a woolly surface when cut, especially with scrapers. The coarse, open-grained texture is not something that turners need to worry about – it cuts nicely with all tools, as long as they are sharp and a slow rate of traverse is used. There is only a slight blunting effect on the cutting edges. Honing will have a positive effect on the surface finish off the tool.

Despite its fairly coarse texture, ash is often used to produce utilitarian pieces for domestic use. Its high resistance to shock makes it ideal for making handles for such things as turning tools and mallets.

It sands easily, using either a dry or a wet sanding method, and can be finished to a high polish with both penetrative and surface finishes. It lends itself to the technique of staining the wood, then filling the open grain with a contrasting 'liming' or paste wax.

Hint

If liming wax is to be used as a finish, open the grain first with a bronze brush (also called a suede brush), then seal the dyed or natural wood with a sanding sealer, and sand prior to using the liming paste or wax

Closed form in figured ash by John Hunnex

Lignum vitae
Guaiacum officinale

Other names
Ironwood,
palo santo,
guayacán,
guayacán negro

Two woodworking mallets, the
right-hand one dated 1921

**Possible
health
risks**
Dermatitis

Grows
Central America, Caribbean,
Venezuela, Colombia
Height 20ft (6m)
Trunk diameter 1ft (0.3m)
Specific gravity 1.23
Typical dry weight 77lb/ft³
(1230kg/m³)

Seasoning
The wood is quite difficult to season
and requires a lot of care. If left in
the round or in large thicknesses, it
never really dries. End-coating is
recommended to prevent shakes and
end splits. If producing artistic work
such as bowls, boxes and so on,
rough-turning followed by further
seasoning is recommended, but it can
be turned wet or part-seasoned if
accuracy is not required.

Description

The heartwood is a greenish-brown colour, or sometimes nearly black. Its grain is irregular and strongly interlocked, with a very uniform, fine texture; it is capable of holding very fine detail without breaking out. About a third of the wood's weight is guaiac gum, which makes it feel oily or waxy. The sapwood is distinct from the heartwood and is a creamy or pale yellow colour. The wood darkens somewhat over time, with exposure to light.

The wood is exceptionally dense, heavy and hard, which makes it an excellent choice for mallet heads, especially those of carving pattern. Its oily nature and natural self-lubricating properties have made it a valuable commodity for ships' propeller bearings – it has three times the life of steel or bronze. Being very dense, it is suitable for thread chasing, but is not as good as boxwood (*Buxus sempervirens*) or African blackwood (*Dalbergia melanoxylon*).

The gum in the wood can stick to blades and cutting edges, especially those of bandsaws and circular saws, which makes cutting it a little tricky; it also has a slight dulling effect.

It is usually only available in small sizes, commonly in pre-dimensioned billets.

Working qualities

Lignum vitae's irregular and interlocking grain is sometimes prone to tearing or pulling out. When cutting with a gouge, you will more often than not get small chips and a bit of dust, but not ribbon shavings. Sometimes a better finish can be achieved by using a freshly honed scraper, which may sometimes produce actual shavings. A good finish can be achieved straight from the tool.

Fresh-cut wood or dust has a very distinctive smell to it – a mixture of citrus and eucalyptus. The dust is oily and clings to all surfaces. Because the wood is oily there is likely to be gum build-up on the bevels when using bevel-rubbing tools such as gouges and skews; this will need to be cleaned off periodically to maintain full cutting control.

Sanding is difficult at times. The wood is so hard that it takes a long time to remove any but the smallest of blemishes – far better to get as good a finish as you can off the tool before sanding. Dry sanding is likely to cause heat-checking, and to raise a lot of dust which will gum up the abrasive. Wet sanding, working through to very fine grades of abrasive, is the best way to finish this wood, especially if oil is used as the lubricant – but bear in mind that when sapwood is present there is a risk of colour contamination, so dry-sand instead. The wood's natural oiliness can make it difficult to finish. It resists some surface finishes; a wipe over the sanded surface with cellulose thinners may help. It polishes readily with oils, though they do not penetrate far. A highly lustrous finish can be achieved.

Hint
Try wet-sanding using water as the lubricant, and then buffing with a power-buffing mop loaded with a micro-abrasive. The already oily wood will polish to a very high lustre with no additional finish applied

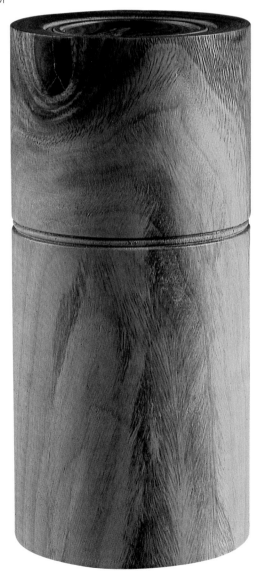

Box by Mark Baker

Bubinga
Guibourtia demeusei

Other names
African rosewood, akume, essingang, buvenga, ovang, waka, okweni; rotary-cut veneers are known as **kevasingo**

Oiled finish

Possible health risks
Dermatitis and skin lesions

Grows
Central and west central tropical Africa
Height 70ft (21m)
Trunk diameter 4ft (1.2m)
Specific gravity .88
Typical dry weight 55lb/ft³ (880kg/m³)

Seasoning
This wood seasons reasonably well, with little degrade, but the gum sometimes causes problems. It is advisable to season it slowly to prevent distortion and checking. Rough-turning, followed by further seasoning, works well to minimize distortion and gives more predictable results than air-drying the wood in board form. On highly figured pieces it may be prudent to coat the end grain or the whole piece with PVA to even out the drying process.

Kiln-drying works well when flat boards are required, especially for platters or cabinetry work.

Description

Bubinga is a dense, hard and wonderfully decorative wood. The sapwood is normally greyish-white, ivory or streaked ivory-white, or sometimes brownish-white. The heartwood is altogether different, featuring light to medium reds, orange-browns and mid-toned browns, often with lighter veining in red or purple. The grain is normally straight or interlocked, and the annual rings are conspicuous. Fine pores, which can contain a reddish gum, may be found throughout. The texture is variable: it may be coarse but is usually fine to medium, and the surface can be highly lustrous. The wood will darken a lot over time, losing the orange-red vibrancy and mellowing down to a mid-brown tone. The grain pattern, which varies greatly from piece to piece, will remain distinct.

Because it contains silica, it has a medium to severe blunting effect on cutting edges. It is available in large sizes, giving turners a lot of scope to experiment with different types of project.

Working qualities

Bubinga cuts well with all tools; occasionally the interlocking grain will pluck out, but sharp tools and a delicate cut will usually solve this. There is also a risk of splintering at the edges; a gentle cut will prevent this, but be careful when using a scraper near the edge. A standard cut with a freshly honed scraper will help remove fine ripples, but a shear cut is a better option, and will usually remove any minor grain blemishes or tear-out as well. The wood can produce long shavings, but is more likely to give short, curly shavings with some very fine, irritant dust. It can be brittle at the edges, where chunks of wood may break away. Gentle cuts with a sharp tool will minimize this.

It sands well, but will clog up abrasive if sanded dry. It wet-sands well, as long as no sapwood is present to cause colour contamination. It can be taken to a high lustre with both surface and penetrative finishes.

Box in figured bubinga by Chris Stott

Holly

Ilex aquifolium and *I. opaca*

Other names

European holly (*I. aquifolium*), American holly (*I. opaca*). There are many different species of holly worldwide

Box by Chris Stott

Possible health risks
Not known

Grows

Europe and western Asia (*I. aquifolium*), USA (*I. opaca*)
Height 40–70ft (12–21m)
Trunk diameter 1–2ft (0.3–0.6m)
Specific gravity .80
Typical dry weight 50lb/ft³ (800kg/m³)

Seasoning

This wood is best cut in the winter to minimize discoloration. It is not easy to season and is highly likely to end-split and distort if it is dried in the round; worse still, it may split radially all the way along. If you rough-turn holly, allow an extra ¼–⅜in wall thickness per 12in diameter (6–10mm per 300mm) to compensate for the large movement, and coat the rough-turned piece with PVA before setting it aside to season slowly. Do allow plenty of airflow, or blue staining is likely to occur. The wood dries better if it is cut into small stock and weighted down.

Description

Holly is a hard, heavy and dense wood. The sapwood is usually just a tiny bit whiter than the heartwood, and they both range from creamy-white to ivory in colour. The wood normally has no figure, and the fine, close grain is irregular and even-textured, with the ability to hold very fine detail. The colour does darken with age and exposure, so finishes with UV inhibitors are recommended to minimize this.

Because it splits readily when seasoning, it is not usually available in large sizes, unless it is bought as a log and cut to your own requirements. Holly is a great wood for wet turning: it distorts a lot, and some fantastic shapes are possible. It is mostly used for decorative or artistic pieces, but is also suitable for utilitarian turnings.

Working qualities

The wood cuts easily when wet, producing long ribbon shavings as most woods do. When seasoned, the irregular grain can make cutting a little difficult, but usually it is well-behaved and pleasant to turn. Grain tear-out is a possibility, but this can usually be obviated by making cuts with a freshly honed gouge. Conventional scraping often causes damage, so very gentle cuts in shear-scraping mode are recommended; but bevel-rubbing tools definitely produce the finest results. Holly sands well; a better and finer finish is achieved using the wet sanding method – dry sanding is OK but produces more dust. This is a wood that can be carved.

It will take both penetrative and surface finishes, but both types will have a darkening effect on the wood.

Vase by John Hunnex

American black walnut

Juglans nigra

Other names
American walnut, eastern black walnut, gunwood, Virginia walnut

Burr (burl)

Possible health risks
Irritation to eyes and skin

Grows
Canada and USA
Height 70–90ft (21–27m)
Trunk diameter 2–4ft (0.6–1.2m)
Specific gravity .64
Typical dry weight 40lb/ft³
(640kg/m³)

Seasoning
This wood dries slowly, and care has to be taken to avoid degrade. Faults which may occur include checking, iron staining, ring failure, honeycombing and collapse. Kiln-dried and air-dried wood in a variety of sizes are readily available for the construction, architectural and cabinetmaking industries; but if you are producing artistic turnings and want to rough-turn your work, allow ¼in (6mm) or so extra in the wall thickness per 12in (300mm) diameter to compensate for the increased movement. Figured wood should be coated with PVA, either on the end grain or all over, before being set aside to season.

Description

This is a gem of a timber both to look at and to work with. The grain pattern is simply stunning, and it is much sought-after by woodworkers of all kinds. The heartwood colour can range from a light grey-brown to a dark chocolate or purplish-black. The sapwood is naturally whitish-yellow or brown, but can be stained or steamed to match the heartwood. The grain is usually straight and slightly open, but curls or waves may occur. The texture of the wood is generally coarse; the dull lustre develops to a more glossy patina in time. Spectacular figuring is common, including pippy knots, knot clusters, mottled, curly, rippled and wavy figure. Burrs (burls), stumpwood and crotches are areas in which figure is likely to occur – but veneer companies will buy up highly figured trees before other woodworkers get a look-in.

This is an excellent candidate for wet turning, where the wood is turned to a thin wall thickness and then allowed to 'move' freely. It is also a good choice if you want to use carving on your turned work. It is available in large sizes, so there are many possibilities. American walnut is used in joinery and cabinetmaking, and for artistic and utilitarian turning.

Working qualities
It cuts beautifully whether wet or seasoned; a very fine finish can be achieved off the tool, although it does have a distinct blunting effect on cutting edges. The slightly open grain does not present a problem, but grain filling may be necessary, especially in cabinet work, to produce an ultra-fine finish. It cuts well with all tools, but very gentle cuts are necessary with a scraper to prevent tear-out. Old wood tends to be very dusty, but freshly seasoned timber produces nice curly shavings with very little dust. The dust is noxious, so deal with it in an appropriate manner to avoid ingestion.

Burrs and rippled wood can tear out a little more than the plain wood, but gentle cuts with very sharp tools soon make light work of any potential problems. American walnut carves beautifully with either hand or power tools.

The wood sands well with both wet and dry sanding methods, although wet sanding should be avoided when sapwood is present, because of the risk of colour contamination. It readily accepts both surface and penetrative finishes, and a very high gloss can be achieved.

Hint
Sharpen or hone tools regularly to achieve the best finish possible straight from the cutting edge

Hollow form
by John Hunnex

European walnut

Juglans regia

Other names
Usually differentiated according to origin: Persian, French, Black Sea, etc. walnut

Burr (burl)

Ripple figure

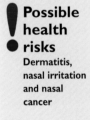
Possible health risks
Dermatitis, nasal irritation and nasal cancer

Grows
Europe, Turkey, south-west Asia
Height 100ft (30m)
Trunk diameter 2–3ft (0.6–0.9m)
Specific gravity .64
Typical dry weight 40lb/ft³ (640kg/m³)

Seasoning
This wood dries well but can take a long time. Air-dried wood is most commonly available, but kiln-dried stock can be found. Honeycombing can occur in larger stock if it is dried too quickly. Allow an extra ¼in (6mm) or so of wall thickness per 12in (300mm) diameter when rough-turning to take movement into account. Spindles, balusters and other such work can be made from kiln- or air-dried timber of about 10–12% moisture content.

Description

This is a stunning wood to look at. The heartwood is normally greyish-brown with some irregular dark streaking. The sapwood is paler, and clearly different from the heartwood. The colour mellows quite a bit with time, but the grain pattern remains distinct. European walnut is a medium-dense wood which usually has straight grain but can also be wavy. It has a coarse texture, and a clearly defined central core can sometimes produce a piece of beautifully figured wood. Walnut crotch, burr (burl) and stumpwood can also produce attractive figuring, but highly figured trees are likely to be snapped up by veneer manufacturers.

Working qualities

This wood works very similarly to American black walnut (*J. nigra*). It has a moderate blunting effect on cutting tools and is an ideal candidate for wet turning (though the finish off the tool can be a bit woolly), as well as being excellent to work when seasoned. Seasoned wood cuts well with gouges and skews, permitting a nice finish off the tool. It scrapes well, unless it is highly figured – in which case you may experience grain tear-out or woolliness with all but the most delicate of shear cuts. Walnut carves well with either hand or power tools.

Square-turned platter
by Mark Baker

Wet and dry sanding both produce excellent results, the former giving a slightly finer finish and less dust. As with American walnut, the dust is unpleasant (as all dust is, for that matter), so proper precautions should be taken to prevent inhalation.

Both penetrative and surface finishes work well on walnut, although it may be necessary to fill the grain, or to cut back between multiple coats of surface finish, in order to achieve a flat, smooth surface.

African mahogany

Khaya ivorensis and related species

Other names

Akuk, bandoro, bisselon, eri kiree, ogwango, undianunu, n'gollon, zaminguila, oganwo, acajou. Related species include *K. anthotheca*, *K. grandifoliola*, *K. senegalensis*, *K. nyasica*

Box by Chris Stott

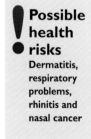

Possible health risks
Dermatitis, respiratory problems, rhinitis and nasal cancer

Grows

Tropical areas of west, central and east Africa

Height 110–140ft (33–43m)
Trunk diameter 6ft (1.8m)
Specific gravity .53
Typical dry weight 33lb/ft³ (530kg/m³)

Seasoning

This wood dries very quickly and hardly degrades, but if reaction or tension wood is present it will distort a lot. Kiln-drying and air-drying are both acceptable methods for seasoning. However, when turning items other than spindle work for architectural applications – for which kiln-dried timber will be sufficient – rough-turning followed by further seasoning is recommended.

Description

Turners often overlook this pleasant wood in favour of the unrelated American or true mahogany (*Swietenia macrophylla*), which comes from South America. This is a shame, as African mahogany is a nice wood to work with. When freshly cut it is usually a light pinkish-brown, but as it is exposed to light it darkens to a deep red and can often take on a purple tinge. It darkens greatly with age, to an almost uniform mid-brown.

The grain can be straight, but is usually interlocked, producing a striped or roey figure on quartersawn surfaces, and crotch and swirl figures are often present. The texture is variable, sometimes being coarse with a high, golden lustre, and at other times fine; this appears to depend on where the tree grew. The sapwood is usually creamy-white to yellow, but sometimes it is not easily distinguished from the heartwood. The wood is prone to thunder shakes, especially in figured logs.

It is a medium-dense wood, available in large sizes. Often used by joiners and cabinetmakers, it is particularly suited for architectural work such as balusters and spindles, as well as being a good choice for table legs and so on. It is also appropriate for artistic and decorative pieces.

Working qualities

This is a nice wood to work with. It cuts well with sharp tools; gouges and skews produce nice curly shavings with very little dust. The end grain can tear out a little if too much pressure is used during the cut, or if the tools are blunt. Shear-scraping is an excellent method for cleaning up any minor blemishes, and is superior to conventional scraping for this wood. However, the variable grain can sometimes make the cut a little woolly, especially when scraping. The wood carves well, but best results are obtained with power tools.

It sands well with both wet and dry sanding methods, but wet-sand only if no sapwood is present. It readily takes both penetrative and surface finishes. It can be polished or buffed to a high lustre.

Hint

Be careful when sanding detail on spindles. Over-aggressive sanding or inattention to what you are doing will result in the rounding-over and softening of crisp detail, spoiling the clarity which sets hand turning apart from machine turning

Dish by John Hunnex

Osage-orange
Maclura pomifera

Other names
Bow wood,
bodare, bodark,
bois d'arc,
hedge,
hedge apple,
horse apple,
naranjo chino,
mock-orange,
osage

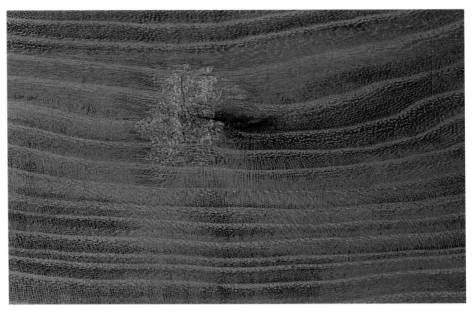

Grows
USA
Height 50ft (15m)
Trunk diameter 2ft (0.6m)
Specific gravity .76
Typical dry weight 48lb/ft³
(760kg/m³)

Description
Osage-orange is dense, very hard and resilient. The heartwood when freshly cut varies from greenish-yellow or golden-yellow to bright orange with darker streaks. When exposed to light it will darken to a uniform The sapwood is a light yellow and is easily distinguished from the heartwood. The wood usually has a close, straight grain, but it can be interlocking or irregular; the texture is somewhat coarse. It is used by turners for decorative and artistic items, but also has many applications in construction work.

Seasoning
This wood seasons well with both kiln- and air-drying methods. It will move a little during the drying process. The rough-turning method of drying and stabilizing wood works well for this timber, but it can also be wet-turned to completion.

 Possible health risks
Not known

Working qualities

I am fond of this wood; it can be problematic to use, but I think the results are worth the effort. It has a severe blunting effect on the cutting edges of bandsaw blades and turning tools, so frequent sharpening is necessary to achieve a good cut. Like most woods, it cuts more easily wet than seasoned, but in both cases you may experience some problems if you encounter interlocking grain; this is highly likely to tear out if you use anything but the most slow and delicate of cuts with a sharp gouge, followed by abrasives. Scraping will exacerbate the problem of torn grain, so try to deal with it using a gouge. If the grain is straight, however, scrapers can be used to remove any surface undulations, either in conventional or in shear-scraping mode. The wood is suitable for carving, preferably with power tools, though it does not hold very fine detail. It can be somewhat brittle at times, and splintering may occur at the edges of the work.

The wood sands easily, but produces a lot of dust if sanded dry. Wet sanding with water or oil as a lubricant works well, as long as there is no sapwood present to cause colour contamination.

It will readily accept both penetrative and surface finishes. The somewhat coarse, open texture of the wood may need filling prior to finishing, if a perfectly smooth surface is required.

Hint
Use a water-based lacquer finish with UV inhibitors. This will not darken the wood as much as oil- or polyurethane-based finishes

Flask box with inserts of violet rosewood (*Dalbergia louvelli*) by Chris Stott

Wengé
Millettia laurentii

Other names
Awoung,
bokonge, dikela,
mibotu,
nson-so,
palissandre du
Congo

Grows
Congo, Cameroon, Gabon, Tanzania,
Mozambique
Height 50–60ft (15–18m)
Trunk diameter 2ft 6in–3ft
(0.75–1m)
Specific gravity .88
Typical dry weight 55lb/ft^3
(880kg/m^3)

! **Possible
health
● risks**
Dermatitis,
giddiness,
drowsiness,
visual problems,
stomach
cramps;
irritation of the
eyes, skin and
respiratory
systems;
splinters go
septic

Seasoning
This wood seasons quite slowly and
is fairly difficult to dry. It is highly
prone to surface checking and has a
slight tendency to distort. It shows
a small amount of movement in use.
The technique of rough-turning
followed by further seasoning works
well, but is only necessary for artistic
work; kiln-dried wood will be fine for
furniture and joinery items.

Description
This is a dense, heavy wood of striking
appearance, with a clear differentiation
between the white to pale yellow
sapwood and the dark brown heartwood
with fine, close, near-black veins and white
or cream lines. The grain is fairly straight,
and it has a medium to coarse texture
with a low lustre. The wood darkens to a
much deeper brown on exposure, but the
veins remain distinct.

The wood has a small to moderate
blunting effect on cutting edges. It is
available in reasonable sizes, mostly as
dimensioned boards or pre-cut bowl
blanks; it is rarely found as blanks or
sections suitable for large hollow forms, or
as trunks which can be cut to suit one's
own requirements. Because it is so dark,
large pieces can look very imposing and
sombre. You will often find wengé used as
an accent, to set off another, lighter wood;
it is also used for turned components in
joinery and cabinetmaking. It is capable of
holding quite fine detail.

Working qualities

Wengé is not the easiest wood to work, but is worth persevering with because few other woods offer such a fine display of contrasting markings combined with the deep brown colour. It cuts reasonably well with all tools – bevel-rubbing tools giving a slightly better finish – but long shavings are rare. It is more common to achieve small chips and a fair amount of dust – unless the wood has a high moisture content, in which case slightly larger, curly shavings are possible and there is less dust. The wood tends to splinter at the edges of the work; a light, slow cut will solve this problem. The dust is unpleasant and very fine, so extract it properly as close to source as possible to prevent inhalation or ingestion.

This is not a wood that I would recommend for wet-turning and allowing it to move. That is not to say that it will not work (and you may want to set a trend!), but it is more common to season and stabilize it fully before finish-turning. It can be carved, preferably with power tools.

Wengé is prone to heat-checking when sanding. Dry sanding gives off lots of dust, while wet sanding produces a slurry that fills the pores and diminishes the fine, light markings which are such a distinctive feature of the grain. On balance, I would recommend dry sanding, using fresh abrasives and a light touch so as not to generate too much heat. Efficient dust extraction is essential.

The wood can be finished with both penetrative and surface finishes, but the open, coarse grain may need filling for an ultra-smooth feel. I find the open texture pleasant and like the tactile quality of it, so I do not fill the grain; instead I oil and buff with a power buff. Give it a try and see what you think.

Hint
Wengé is a great wood to combine with maple (*Acer* spp.) or ash (*Fraxinus* spp.)

Bowl by Bert Marsh

European olive

Olea europaea

Other names
None.
Related to East
African olive
(*O. hochstetteri*),
which is a
much larger
tree

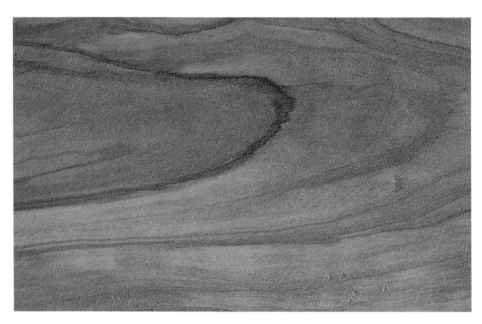

Oiled finish

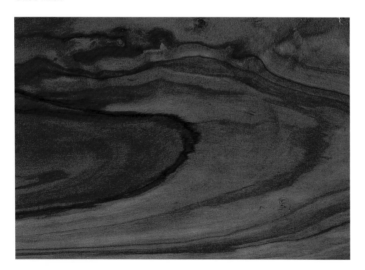

Grows
Mediterranean region, Middle East and North Africa
Height 25ft (8m) max.
Trunk diameter typically 1ft (0.3m) but can reach 3ft (0.9m)
Specific gravity .80
Typical dry weight 50lb/ft³ (800kg/m³)

Seasoning
The wood dries very slowly and has a tendency to warp, check, split and honeycomb if you try to rush it, especially when dried in the round or in large pieces. Large sections will need part-turning followed by further seasoning. I have only ever encountered air-dried wood, which varies greatly in moisture content. The logs and branches are variable in quality and need checking over very carefully; they are rarely free from minor splits or checks. Pre-dimensioned timber, though more expensive, does give you a clearer idea of what you are purchasing.

I use olive mainly for wet turning: it responds well to being turned thin and then allowed to distort freely, with or without bark. Conversely, it can be rough-turned, coated with PVA and set aside to season – but expect some failures.

Description

This is a truly stunning timber: strong, hard, heavy and oily, with a clear differentiation between sapwood and heartwood. The sapwood is gold or creamy-yellow, and often striped. The heartwood is usually tan, pale brown or yellow-brown, and it can be streaked with black, grey or brown. The grain is close and shallowly interlocked, with a fine, even texture which is capable of holding fine detail. Figuring may appear on tangential surfaces. The annual rings are clearly seen. Olive is not usually available in large sizes, as the tree is invariably stumpy and gnarled. The wood is essentially a by-product of the olive-oil industry. Boughs and trunks become available from time to time, but it is more commonly sold as pre-dimensioned blanks.

The shavings will stain your hands and any steel that they come into contact with, so make sure that you clean up thoroughly after using it. The wood has an oily feel which takes a long while to disappear, and a strong smell. Olive can be used by turners for both utilitarian and decorative work.

Working qualities

Wet olivewood is particularly easy and pleasant to work: long ribbon-like shavings positively fly off the tool. The irregular grain does not usually present any problem when working the wood wet. Old or well-seasoned wood is a different matter: the interlocking, irregular grain often plucks out and the edges of the work are liable to splinter. Sharp tools and a slow, deliberate cut will usually overcome this difficulty. Boxes with finials should always be made from straight-grained wood; any cross or interlocking grain in the finial will cause problems and may result in breakage.

The wood is prone to heat-checking, so take care when sanding not to generate too much hear. It is liable to clog the abrasive if you sand it dry, but responds well to wet sanding and can be brought to a fine finish with abrasives. The oils in the wood tend to make it resistant to some surface finishes, but it takes penetrative finishes well.

Hint
Wipe it over with acetone or cellulose thinners prior to applying a surface finish, to ensure a good hold

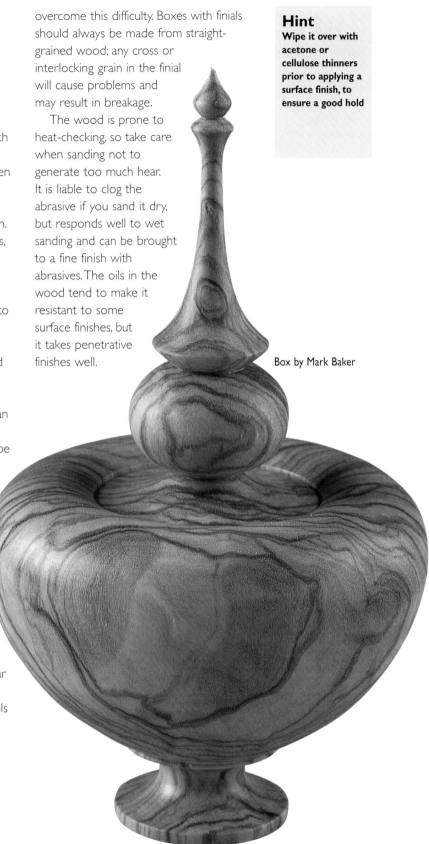

Box by Mark Baker

Purpleheart

Peltogyne porphyrocardia and related species

Other names
Amaranth,
amarante,
guarabu,
morado,
nazareno,
pau roxo,
saka, tananeo,
violetwood

Oiled finish

Possible health risks
Dust can cause irritation and nausea

Grows
Central America and northern South America
Height 100–150ft (30–45m)
Trunk diameter 2–4ft (0.6–1.2m)
Specific gravity .86
Typical dry weight 54lb/ft^3 (860kg/m^3)

Seasoning
This wood usually dries fairly quickly with little degrade, but it can sometimes warp or split. The moisture content in the centre of thicker stock can be a problem, so if you are making bowls, boxes, hollow forms and platters you will get better results by rough-turning it and then setting it aside to season further before final turning. Coating the end grain with PVA will even out the drying and minimize the risk of splitting or surface checking.

Description

This is a wood that you certainly cannot overlook when you see it. Newly cut heartwood is a dull, soft brown colour, but on exposure to light it changes to a bright purple. Sadly, this is a wood that loses its vibrancy of colour, mellowing down to a purplish mid-brown tone. There can also be some difference in colour between one board and another within each species, and minerals in the wood may cause uneven colour. The grain is typically straight but can be roey, wavy, interlocked or irregular. It has a medium to fine, even texture and a high lustre, and is capable of holding quite fine detail. The heartwood is clearly distinct from the sapwood, being an off-white colour.

It is available in large sizes, either as pre-dimensioned blanks or as boards of varying thickness, so a wide variety of work can be created from it. However, large turnings in purpleheart can be quite imposing and 'in your face', so choose your projects wisely. Try smaller bowls, hollow forms or boxes, then work your way up to larger pieces and see what you think. Purpleheart is also a good choice as an accent or contrasting colour against a lighter or darker wood.

Working qualities

Purpleheart is a not as easy to turn as some of the woods featured in this book. It is somewhat brittle, so is liable to splinter, especially near the edges of work, and any irregular or interlocking grain is likely to tear out. Sharp gouges, used on seasoned wood with a slow, delicate cut, will normally produce chips with a small amount of dust but not too much tear-out. Use shear-scraping rather than conventional scraping when possible, to minimize the risk of plucking out the fibres of the wood. If you find that scraping does not improve the surface after the gougework, make a fine finishing cut with the gouge and then go straight to abrasives.

It is prone to heat-checking, and abrasives clog up quickly when the wood is sanded dry, so clean them regularly to prevent heat build-up. Wet sanding works well. If you want any chance of keeping the purple colour for any length of time, use a finish which incorporates a UV inhibitor. However, the wood does finish well with either penetrative or surface finishes.

Box by Chris Stott

Imbuia

Phoebe porosa

Other names
Amarela,
Brazilian walnut,
imbuya,
canella imbuia,
embuia

Figured sample

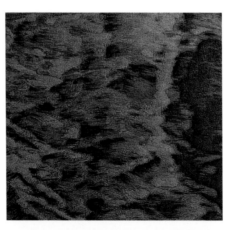

Grows
Southern Brazil
Height 130ft (40m)
Trunk diameter 6ft (1.8m)
Specific gravity .66
Typical dry weight 41lb/ft³
(660kg/m³)

The same sample
with an oiled finish

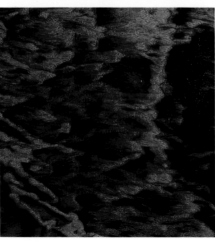

**! Possible
health
● risks**
**The sawdust
can be an
irritant to the
nose, eyes and
skin**

Seasoning
Imbuia is very quick to dry. It is
prone to warp unless care is taken,
and thicker stock has a tendency to
honeycomb and collapse. Movement
in use is medium to small. If you plan
to rough-turn a piece and set it aside
to season, consider coating either the
end grain or the whole item with
thinned-down PVA to even out the
drying process.

Description

There can be considerable colour variation, the heartwood ranging from yellow-green through orange to chocolate brown, with variegated streaks and stripes. The grain is usually straight but it is often curly or wavy, and this produces a fine ribbon figure. This reasonably hard, heavy, dense wood is capable of holding fine detail. It may have quilted, burry (burled) or blistered figuring, and clusters of pippy burr may be found. It has a medium to fine texture and is naturally very lustrous. This wood is very similar to American walnut (*Juglans nigra*) in appearance, but has a finer texture. It mellows quickly to a mid-brown or deep brown colour, but the grain pattern remains distinct. Turners use imbuia mainly for decorative or artistic work, but it also has applications in joinery and cabinetwork.

Working qualities

This wood is unlikely to present any problems when turning. Seasoned wood cuts well with bevel-rubbing tools, producing small shavings with some dust. Freshly honed scrapers produce a nice surface finish. Interlocking grain, when present, does not seem to present any major problems, and can be dealt with easily by delicate cuts with a sharp gouge or scraper.

The burr and quilted forms, however, do present an increased risk of grain tear-out when cutting. To lessen this risk, try to get as good a finish as you can straight from a gouge rather than using a scraper, then go straight to abrasives.

Abrasives – even those with a stearate coating to reduce clogging – are liable to clog quickly when dry-sanding, but a nice finish is achieved as long as the abrasives are cleaned regularly. Wet sanding is also an option. Both penetrative and surface finishes can be used with good results, though oil-based finishes have a considerable darkening effect. The wood can be power-buffed to a very high lustre.

Hint

Since finishes have a big impact on the visual and tactile feel of a piece of work, try out the finish you would like to use on a waste piece of wood beforehand just to make sure you like the result. I like oil for unfigured imbuia. For figured pieces I prefer a surface finish of thinned-down melamine lacquer which is then power-buffed. Both finishes show off the grain pattern well

Bowl by Bert Marsh

Snakewood

Piratinera guianensis, syn. Brosimum guianense

Other names

Letterwood, letterhout, amourette, gateado, palo de oro, burokoro, cacique carey, leopardwood, speckled wood

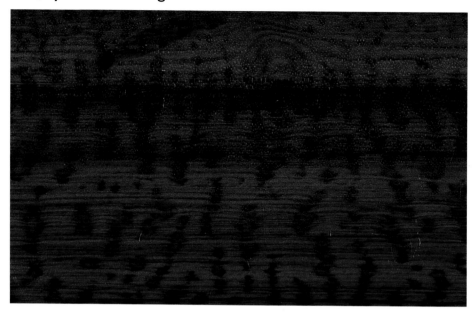

Possible health risks

Thirst, salivation, respiratory tract irritation and nausea

Grows

Central America and tropical South America

Height 80ft (25m)

Diameter of trunk 1–3ft (0.3–0.9m)

Specific gravity 1.30

Dry weight 81lb/m³ (1300kg/m³)

Seasoning

Drying can be difficult, and there may be warping and degrade. Snakewood shows medium movement in use. I strongly recommend rough-turning the blank and coating it with PVA adhesive to even out the moisture loss and minimize checking and warping, and then setting it aside to season further before finish-turning. It can be turned wet or partially seasoned for items such as bowls, but lidded boxes will need to be rough-turned to ensure stability. Snakewood is not available in very large sizes. It can be bought as logs or as a whole tree trunk, but frequently exhibits splits. It is more commonly sold as pre-dimensioned blanks. However you purchase it, store it in an area with a uniform moisture content and temperature to minimize checking.

Description

This wood is naturally high in resin and has markings resembling snakeskin or a spotty leopard – hence its alternative names. The heartwood is dark red to red-brown, with irregular black spots or stripes, which can appear on their own or with interspersed speckles. The wood will darken with time, but the black markings will always remain distinct. The border between heartwood and sapwood is irregular. The sapwood is thick, creamy or yellow-white, and is rarely used because it often contains splits. When a piece is found without splits, it can be used to provide an effective contrast with the darker heartwood. The grain is moderately fine, uniform and straight, with a medium to high lustre.

This dense, hard and heavy wood – one of the heaviest that a turner is likely to encounter – is capable of holding very fine detail. Because it is very expensive, it is usually used for artistic turning, often in small pieces as an accent to a larger piece of wood. I have seen snakewood inserts used to good effect in box lids.

Working qualities

This is a wonderful wood to turn. A fine finish can be achieved with all sharp tools. Because it is naturally resinous, a high shine is produced with bevel-rubbing tools such as gouges and skews. Cutting with these tools produces small chips instead of shavings, with a little dust. Longer shavings can be obtained by using a scraper, in either the conventional or the shear-scraping mode; again the shaving will be fine and accompanied by a little dust.

Snakewood is prone to heat-checking on the end grain, so be careful when sanding. Wet sanding is the better option, as long as no sapwood is present to cause colour contamination. Dry sanding will result in the production of a lot of nasty dust, as well as regular clogging of the abrasive with the wood's natural resin. The high resin content can resist surface finishes, but wiping over with a solvent first should sort the problem out. Alternatively, use oil or wax as a finish and power-buff it to a fine lustre.

Hint

If you make small boxes with this wood the edges can be very hard and sharp. Always run a very fine piece of abrasive over the corner of the foot and rim to 'kill' the sharp edges so that everything is nice to the touch

Box by Chris Stott

Poplar
Populus spp.

Other names
The numerous species known as 'poplar' include European black poplar (*P. nigra*), black Italian poplar (*P. canadensis*), robusta (*P. robusta*), Swedish, Finnish, etc. aspen (*P. tremula*), white poplar (*P. alba*)

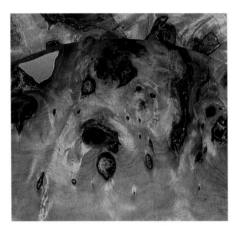

Burr (burl)

Ripple figure

! Possible health ● risks
Asthma, dermatitis, bronchitis, sneezing, eye irritation

Grows
UK and mainland Europe, North America
Height 100–115ft (30–35m)
Trunk diameter 3–4ft (0.9–1.2m), but varies according to species
Specific gravity .45
Typical dry weight 28lb/ft³ (450kg/m³), varying according to species

Seasoning

Poplar dries reasonably quickly with little degrade, but is liable to retain pockets of moisture. The knots are prone to split, but otherwise it will respond to kiln- or air-drying, or to the rough-turning method. If you are undertaking architectural work – balusters, stair spindles and so on – kiln-dried wood will be fine; but for items such as bowls, boxes or vases it is advisable to rough-turn and set aside for further seasoning. Poplar can be turned wet to a thin, even wall thickness to good effect, but is not one of the best choices if you want the work to move a lot as it dries. The burr variants are probably better for this, as they will move a great deal more than the non-figured wood. The surface of wet-turned wood may be woolly, requiring quite a bit of sanding to remove blemishes.

Description

I really love working with this wood, although it is not as widely used as it could be. The colour range is very variable across the related species, from off-white or creamy-white to grey with green tinges, pinkish-brown, or very pale brown with red tinges. It is usually straight-grained with a fine, even texture. It is a soft to medium-density wood that can be a bit woolly. It is used for turned components in the construction and joinery industries, but more commonly for decorative or utilitarian ware.

Turners can make use of the wide variety of available sizes, some of which are large. Poplar produces lovely burrs, which vary in figure from 'pippy', with a mass of knots, through to swirling grain. Rippling can also occur.

Working qualities

When working with seasoned or dry wood, try to get as good a finish as you can using a sharp gouge; if it is not sharp, the finish off the tool is likely to be fluffy. Reasonably long shavings will be produced if the cut is made correctly, and if the wood is freshly seasoned there will be little dust; old stock will produce dust. Poplar's woolly nature can cause a problem if scrapers are used; even in shear-scraping mode, a scraper can cause the fibres to fluff up. Try moving straight on to abrasive after the gouge or skew chisel. It does not splinter in cutting or in use, which makes it a good choice for items used in contact with food.

Poplar sands well with both wet and dry techniques, but be mindful if power-sanding to move the arbor across the work with a very fluid motion. This is always important with power sanding, but poplar is particularly soft and you can quickly create sanding hollows which will mar the surface. Poplar accepts both penetrative and surface finishes well. It can also be stained to accentuate the figuring, but the resulting look may be a little blotchy if care is not taken.

Bowl by Mark Baker

European cherry

Prunus avium

Other names
Gean,
wild cherry,
mazzard,
fruit cherry

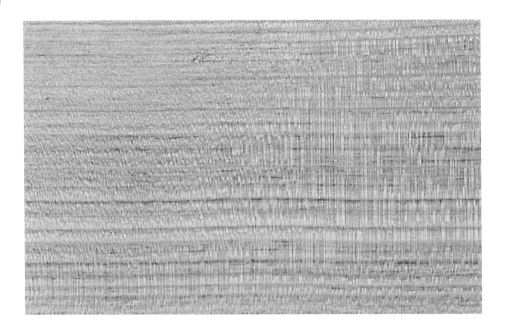

Grows
UK and mainland Europe, western
Asia and North Africa
Height 60–80ft (18–24m)
Trunk diameter 2ft (0.6m)
Specific gravity .61
Typical dry weight 38lb/ft³
(610kg/m³)

Seasoning
Cherry dries quickly but is prone to
warping, and may develop end splits
if not seasoned carefully. The knots
are particularly prone to splitting, but
otherwise it will respond to kiln- or
air-drying or to the rough-turning
technique, provided care is taken not
to dry it too fast. Kiln-dried wood is
sufficient for joinery or cabinetwork
without any further treatment.

Cherry can also be wet-turned to
good effect. The bark is fine enough
to remain in place if you want to
incorporate it into the design.

**Possible
health
risks**
Not known

Description

The heartwood is an orange-red or brown colour and is clearly distinct from the pale cream to buff-white sapwood. When exposed to light, it will lose some of its fresh-cut red hue. Usually straight-grained with a fine and even texture, cherry is a medium-density wood with a very pleasant and clearly defined grain pattern. Burrs (burls) are not uncommon, and ripple or roey figuring can occur. The root structure, if large enough, is also worth considering for turning, though its very high moisture content makes it prone to splitting.

It is available in reasonably large sizes. The largest sizes, obtained by buying a complete section of tree trunk, are particularly suitable for hollow forms; buying a whole section does give you more scope to convert the wood to your own requirements. The wood is suitable both for decorative or artistic work and for utilitarian wares.

Working qualities

All the fruitwoods are a pleasure to work with. They may vary considerably in colour and density, and some have a slightly coarser texture, but all without exception are worth trying. European cherry cuts well when dry, but the grain fibres may fluff up a little when wet-turning it, so make sure the tools being used are sharp. Scrapers may also cause the grain fibres to tear out, especially when wet; but figured areas around knots and so on may be a problem even when dry. Shear-scraping will minimize this, but not prevent it totally.

It sands easily with both wet and dry methods. Surface and penetrative finishes work well and, depending on the finish used, the wood can be brought to a very fine surface. It also stains well, but you may have to clean and degrease the surface with cellulose thinners or other solvent prior to applying the stain or dye.

Hint

Consider using a surface finish such as melamine for work that is not to be used in contact with food. Apply a few coats of thinned-down melamine, allowing each coat to dry, and rubbing down with a fine grade of abrasive (1000–1500 grit) before applying the next coat. Once the final coat is dry, power-buff using a mop loaded with a microfine abrasive held in wax. This will polish the surface and remove any minor blemishes

Bowl by Mark Baker

Amboyna

Pterocarpus indicus

Other names

Philippines or
Solomons
padauk, Papua
New Guinea
rosewood,
yaya sa, narra,
red narra,
yellow narra,
sena, angsena

Burr (burl)

Seasoning

This wood dries quite slowly but shows hardly any degrade; red wood takes longer to season than yellow. It is very stable in use. It responds well to wet turning, but does not move excessively; burrs, however, move unpredictably, so expect localized and erratic distortion. It can also be rough-turned and set aside for further seasoning. When using burr wood, coat the rough-turned piece with PVA before setting it aside to season.

Grows

East Indies

Height 130ft (40m)
Trunk diameter 3ft (1m)
Specific gravity .66
Typical dry weight 41lb/ft³
(660kg/m³)

**Possible
health
risks**
**Dermatitis,
asthma, nausea**

Description

The heartwood ranges from light yellow through golden-yellow to brick red. The sapwood is a light straw colour which complements the heartwood. Amboyna from Cagayan in the Philippines is typically harder, heavier and has a darker, blood-red colour. Sadly, amboyna darkens quite quickly on exposure. The figure can be mottled, fiddleback, curly or rippled as a result of the irregular, crossed and wavy grain. Quartersawn wood can have a ribbon figure, and a flamed figure may appear on flatsawn surfaces. This medium-dense wood is fairly lustrous and has a reasonably fine texture. The burr form is highly sought-after and commands extremely high prices; small pieces are often used very effectively with other timbers to provide a contrasting accent. The shavings are reported to turn water fluorescent blue; I have not tried this, but will with the next batch I get. Turners usually reserve this wood for decorative or artistic work.

Working qualities

The plain form of amboyna works satisfactorily, rather than well: it has a tendency to splinter on the outer edges, and grain tear-out is likely to be experienced, unless you are turning the piece wet. Shear-scraping rather than conventional scraping is likely to reduce the risk of grain tear-out. If the wood is old a lot of dust is produced, so take suitable precautions to control this properly. The burr form, strangely, is not so prone to tear-out, although the tightly clustered knots may cause problems in old wood, and will produce a lot of dust. Freshly seasoned amboyna burr seems to work more easily than plain wood; it is delightful to turn when wet, and will move

or distort to create wonderful 'organic' shapes. The wood carves well with either power or hand tools.

Abrasives clog quite quickly, but a quick clean with a bronze brush (a suede brush) soon sorts that out. A fine finish can be achieved with either wet or dry methods, but if using the wet sanding technique make sure there is no sapwood present to cause colour contamination. The burr form of this wood is prone to heat-checking if excessive heat is generated. Amboyna takes both surface and penetrative finishes well and can be brought to a high lustre. Power buffing will help if a very high-lustre finish is required.

Bowl by Bert Marsh

African padauk
Pterocarpus soyauxii

Other names
Barwood,
bosulu,
camwood,
corail, mbe,
mututi, ngula

Bird-box ornament by
Chris Stott in maple
(*Acer* sp.) and padauk

! Possible health ● risks
**Sawdust can
cause skin and
respiratory
problems,
swelling of the
eyelids, itching
and vomiting**

Grows
Tropical west and central Africa
Height 100–130ft (30–40m)
Trunk diameter 2–4ft (0.6–1.2m)
or wider
Specific gravity .72
Typical dry weight 45lb/ft³
(720kg/m³)

Seasoning
This wood dries with hardly any
degrade and shows little movement
in use. It can be wet-turned and
finished straight away, but because it
is usually supplied as through-cut
boards rather than logs it is more
common to convert it into blanks
first, then rough-turn it and set it
aside to stabilize before finish-turning.
Kiln-dried wood is fine for
architectural or furniture turnings.

Description

This dense wood is one of the most strikingly coloured ones that turners are likely to encounter. It is capable of holding quite fine detail without breaking out. When the wood is freshly cut the heartwood is a bold red-orange, but it will change over a period of time to a strong red or pink-red with dark streaks. It can darken even further to a red-purple, or even black. The colour will later fade with age, losing the bright red and mellowing to a mid reddish-brown tone. The grain ranges from straight to interlocked, with a fine to medium texture and a natural surface lustre. The sapwood is easily differentiated from the heartwood: when freshly cut it is white, but it will turn grey-brown or yellow after a time on exposure to light. African padauk is available in very large sizes, giving the turner a lot of scope to experiment.

Working qualities

At some stage or other you are likely to have the opportunity to turn this lovely wood. It is a nice wood to work, and cuts cleanly if the tools are sharp and used sensitively; you may well be able to get a fine finish straight off the tool that requires very little sanding. It has a slight blunting effect on cutting edges, so honing may be advisable, but you should not need to resort to the grinder too often. It carves well with both hand and power carving tools.

The worst aspect of this wood is the peppery dust it produces. There is a lot of it, and it is sticky, clinging to almost everything it touches; it can stain clothes and hands, and needs to be extracted as close to the source as possible.

Good results are achieved with either the dry or the wet sanding method – but avoid wet sanding if sapwood is present, or you will cause colour contamination. Penetrative finishes such as oil have a marked darkening effect on this wood. If you wish to retain the vibrant red colour, consider a surface finish with a UV inhibitor in it; this will not prevent colour loss completely, but will slow it down.

Hint

After turning, shower as soon as you can to remove the dust created during the day. The longer you are in contact with any kind of wood dust, the more likely you are to experience reactions to it

Hollow form
by John Hunnex

Pear

Pyrus communis

Other names
Common pear,
pearwood,
peartree,
wild pear,
choke pear

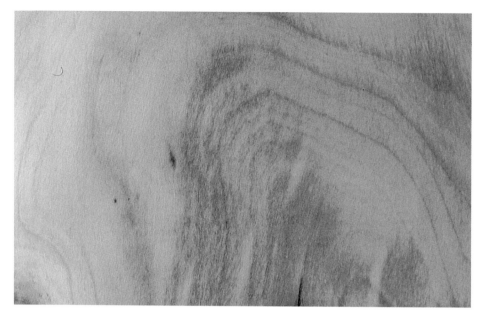

Steamed

Seasoning
This wood is slow-drying and has tendencies to warp and distort if the stacks are not held down under weights. Gentle kiln-drying is recommended, and is more effective than air-drying, which will more likely than not result in splitting. Pear can either be rough-turned and set aside to season further, or wet-turned to completion. Wet-turned pieces can sometimes distort quite a lot.

Grows
UK and mainland Europe, western Asia and USA
Height 30–40ft (9–12m)
Trunk diameter 1–2ft (0.3–0.6m)
Specific gravity .70
Typical dry weight 44lb/ft³ (700kg/m³)

Possible health risks
Not known

Description

The heartwood can range from light pinkish-cream tones through soft orange-reds to a pale pinkish-brown, which can be altered by steaming to a more intense pink. Steamed pear retains its pink colour for some time before mellowing to a soft coffee-brown; unsteamed wood will mellow down to a creamy coffee colour with time. This dense wood has a very fine, even texture and is capable of holding intricate, fine detail; it is used for carving the end-grain blocks used in wood engraving, and other small, highly decorative items such as netsuke. The grain of the wood is usually straight. On quartersawn surfaces a mottled figure may sometimes be present. It sometimes forms burrs, although rarely. The roots are sometimes large enough to turn – they have a varied, wild pattern of interlocking grain – but, due to their high moisture content, they suffer badly from splitting and cell collapse during the drying process.

Pear is not readily available in large sizes unless you buy the whole tree, in which case large hollow forms and so on can be created from the trunk and branches. More commonly, small or medium-sized sections are available, which are ideal for utilitarian or artistic work such as bowls, boxes, small hollow forms and goblets. Hollow forms are a real treat to turn in this wood, as are small boxes with finials or other fine details.

Working qualities

This is a wonderful wood to turn or carve, and will not present any problems to a turner who has mastered the basics of how tools cut. It generally cuts best with gouges, though on spindle work the skew will produce a finish second to none; both are capable of giving a finish straight from the tool that may not require any abrasive, though in practice it is more likely that a very light sanding with a fine grade of abrasive will be needed. Scrapers will not give as clean a finish, but if they are used carefully a mid-grade abrasive followed by finer grades will be sufficient to produce a good result. Seasoned pear yields medium-length shavings with very little dust.

The wet timber will produce long ribbons of shavings with sharp tools. Turning dry wood will not present any problems: the wood still cuts cleanly, but the shavings are not so long, and there may be a little dust produced. As long as they are sharp, any tools can produce an excellent finish.

Wet or dry sanding will result in a good surface finish, but dry sanding, if excessive heat is generated, may result in heat-checks appearing on the end grain. Wet-turned pieces should be wet-sanded with water as a lubricant, then rubbed over when dry with very fine abrasive, prior to applying a finish of your choice. Pear accepts readily both surface and penetrative finishes, and can be buffed by hand or power-buffed to a very fine, lustrous finish. Pear is a wood that can be stained, and is a favourite choice for ebonizing.

Hint

If making boxes, try wet-sanding the inside then buffing, and not applying any more finish in that area. This will create a very smooth interior without the risk of any finish getting caught in stored items such as ring settings

Box in steamed pear by Mark Baker

European oak

Quercus robur and *Q. petraea*

Other names

Pedunculate oak (*Q. robur*); sessile oak, durmast oak (*Q. petraea*). Syn. for *Q. robur*: *Q. pedunculata*; for *Q. petraea*: *Q. sessiliflora*

Brown oak

Burr (burl)

Possible health risks

Sneezing, dermatitis, nasal cancer

Grows

UK and mainland Europe, Turkey, North Africa; also south-eastern Canada and north-eastern USA

Height 60–100ft (18–30m)

Trunk diameter 4–6ft (1.2–1.8m)

Specific gravity .72

Typical dry weight 45lb/ft³ (720kg/m³)

Seasoning

This wood is slow to dry, and likely to check, split, warp and honeycomb, especially when air-dried from the natural state. The likelihood of shrinkage is also high. Movement in service is medium. When rough-turning, allow an extra ¼in (6mm) in addition to the standard 1in (25mm) of wall thickness per 12in (300mm) diameter to take into account the likelihood of warping, and coat it with PVA before seasoning. For architectural work, kiln-dried stock is fine. European oak is a great wood for wet-turning to completion – especially the burr forms, which may move a lot as they dry, creating fantastic undulating forms.

Description

A true king among woods, European oak has a heartwood varying in colour from light tan or biscuit to deep chocolate brown. The wood mellows a lot with time and can darken to a deep brown, or take on a reddish or orange-brown tone. It has obvious alternating bands of earlywood and latewood. The sapwood is somewhat lighter, and about 1in (25mm) wide. This is a tough, reasonably heavy, dense wood whose grain is typically straight, but irregularities and cross grain can occur. Though the texture is coarse, it is still capable of holding reasonably fine detail. When the wood is quartersawn the rays and growth rings show a lovely figure with a metallic sheen, known as 'silver grain'.

Brown oak results from fungal attack in the growing tree. It is a deep purplish-brown, and is slightly less strong than ordinary oak. Fungal activity stops when the wood is seasoned.

Oak often forms burrs, which are highly prized by turners and cabinetmakers. The figure in these ranges from small, tight clusters of pippy knots, to whole tightly packed sections of mid-sized knot formations and whorls of swirling grain. The list of uses for this wood is immense, but suffice to say that its availability in large sizes means that turners can use this timber in a variety of ways: architectural items such as columns, spindles and balusters; turnery for cabinetmaking; utilitarian and artistic forms.

Working qualities

Oak cuts well in most situations, but has a moderate to severe blunting effect on cutting edges. Frequent sharpening will be necessary. Occasionally it may splinter off at the edges of the work, or suffer from grain tear-out when there is cross, irregular grain or knots; gentle cuts with very sharp tools are necessary to minimize the risk of this. However, most of the time it will cut very well with gouges,

leaving a fine finish straight off the tool. Scrapers, too, if freshly honed, can produce a good finish, but not so good as gouges or, for that matter, the skew chisel. If the wood is freshly seasoned, it produces little dust when turned. Old wood, however, can generate lots of dust, which is quite choking and has a musty smell. Oak's ability to produce a nice finish straight from the tool is particularly prized by carvers. Many ancient buildings, and furniture both old and new, have turned items or carvings made from oak.

Both surface and penetrative finishes can be used – oil being my favourite finish, as it imparts a nice warm glow to the wood, which improves with every coat. The surface can be buffed, either by hand or by a power-buffing method, to produce a very fine lustre.

The open grain texture makes oak a great candidate for liming; this is usually reserved for furniture and joinery work, but can be used to good effect on turned pieces. The grain is opened with a bronze brush (a suede brush) after turning to completion and sanding. The work is then given a coat of sanding sealer. Once this is dry, liming wax is applied; this penetrates the grain and fills it, contrasting with the natural wood surface.

Hint

Oak burrs can be large, and may move a lot once turned, because of moisture loss and relief of internal stresses. If you are turning them to completion wet or partially seasoned, try leaving the bark or natural edge of the burr intact. When the wood moves it will go out of round; the natural edge draws the eye away from this to a large extent, disguising the distortion

Bowl in burr oak, ebony (*Diospyros* sp.) and leather by John Hunnex

Pink ivory

Rhamnus zeyheri, syn. Berchemia zeyheri

Other names
Red ivory
wood,
pau preto,
umgoloti,
mucarane,
sungangona

Oiled finish

**Possible
health
risks**
Not known

Grows
Mozambique; also southern and
south-eastern Africa
Height 20–40ft (6–12m)
Trunk diameter 7–12in
(0.2–0.3cm)
Specific gravity .90
Typical dry weight 56lb/ft³
(900kg/m³)

Seasoning
This wood is difficult to air-dry, and if
you kiln-dry it you have to take care,
or degrade can be severe. High
differential shrinkage can cause major
distortion, and the wood also shows
large amounts of movement in use.
It can be wet-turned to completion
but, considering the type of projects
usually undertaken with this wood,
it is generally more appropriate to
rough-turn it before further
seasoning, allowing ¼in (6mm) or
more of extra wall thickness per 12in
(300mm) diameter to account for
the high distortion rate.

Description

This beautiful wood is dense, hard and heavy. The heartwood is yellowish-brown to deep red in colour, while the sapwood is off-white to grey. It has straight to interlocked grain with a fine pore structure and a fairly fine and even texture. It has a pinkish striped figure that is created by alternating bands of dark and light wood in the growth rings.

Since it is only available in small sizes, either as precut blanks or as logs, typical uses would include small boxes or hollow forms. When heartwood and sapwood are used in combination, the colour contrast can be very effective. The wood can hold very fine detail. It has a medium to severe blunting effect on cutting edges, and bandsaw blades do not last long when dimensioning this wood. Sadly, the wood loses its pink-red colour in time and mellows down to a soft brown with a pink tinge.

Working qualities

This is a great wood to work with. It cuts well with gouges and scrapers, which produce fine shavings and leave a very fine finish straight off the tool. Skew chisels can be a problem if interlocking grain is present, but light cuts will usually solve this. If the wood is old it can be dusty to work, but it is not usually so. Sharp tools are vital, and they will need frequent sharpening while working this wood. It is dense enough to be used for thread chasing by hand, but if interlocking grain is present there is a risk of the threads fracturing or chipping out. It is also a nice wood to carve with hand or power tools.

Careful sanding is required to avoid heat-checking. Dry and wet sanding methods can be used to good effect, though wet sanding should not be used when sapwood is present, to avoid colour contamination. The grain on wet-turned wood may fluff up a little, so after sanding allow the piece to dry and then sand again by hand prior to applying the finish of your choice. Surface or penetrative finishes can be used, and the wood can be taken to a very high polish.

Hint

Power buffing with a polishing mop loaded with a micro-abrasive will eliminate any superficial blemishes in the finish. This will create a lustrous surface with a silky feel, which can be enhanced further by an application of wax

Bowl by Bert Marsh

False acacia
Robinia pseudoacacia

Other names
Acacia, locust,
black locust,
white locust,
yellow locust,
robinia

Burr (burl),
finished with oil

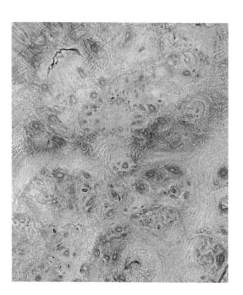

**Possible
health
risks**
The dust can
be an irritant
to the eyes and
skin, and cause
nausea and
malaise

Grows
Mainly Canada and USA; also Asia,
Europe, New Zealand and North
Africa
Height 40–80ft (12–24m)
Trunk diameter 1–2ft (0.3–0.6m)
Specific gravity .72
Typical dry weight 45lb/ft³
(720kg/m³)

Seasoning
This is a slow-drying wood and has a
tendency to warp or distort badly.
There can be end and surface
checking, and it shows medium
movement in use. Minute splits are
frequently found in logs.

This is another wood that may
need an extra ¼in (6mm) or so of
wall thickness added to the standard
1in per 12in diameter (25mm per
300mm) if you are going to rough-
turn and set it aside to season
further. This will allow for the high
distortion rate. It is a wood that can
be wet-turned to completion and
then allowed to distort freely,
although in my experience the
movement is erratic. Wet-turned
burrs take on a 'hammered' effect
due to uneven drying of the knots
and figured areas compared to the
surrounding parts.

Description

The sapwood is thin and yellow, and the heartwood ranges from greenish-yellow to dark or golden-brown. On exposure to light it darkens to golden-brown or russet. The wood has a straight grain with a coarse texture, and shows a marked contrast between the dense latewood and large-pored earlywood. It is a tough wood of medium density, and has a moderate blunting effect on tools.

This wood frequently produces burrs, ranging from tight pippy figuring to violently swirling grain. These burrs are quite stunning and are a great favourite of mine.

Sadly, it is not available in very big sizes, but can be bought in branch or trunk sections, precut blanks or through-cut boards, which gives the turner a lot of scope to experiment.

Working qualities

Both plain and burr forms of this wood are nice to work when wet or partially seasoned. It cuts well, producing long ribbon shavings, and leaves quite a nice finish off the tool, which may require only a light sanding to remove minor blemishes. Seasoned wood is prone to producing small chips and quite a bit of dust. Interlocking grain is likely to pull or tear out, in which case shear-scraping will result in a better finish than conventional scraping. There can be a bit of splintering towards the outer edges of the work, so work carefully with light cuts and sharp tools. This is a wood that can be carved as well as turned, although I prefer to use power carving tools for this.

Sanding can be carried out using either wet or dry methods, and the wood accepts surface or penetrative finishes well. It can be buffed to a very high polish.

Hint

If you find minute splits in the piece, do not despair. Once the primary profile has been achieved, put a spot or two of thin cyanoacrylate adhesive into the crack and immediately sand that area both inside and out while the adhesive is still wet. The glue and the dust will mix together to create a filler which will stick in the split and blend in well. If you let the glue dry before sanding, there will always be an adhesive stain

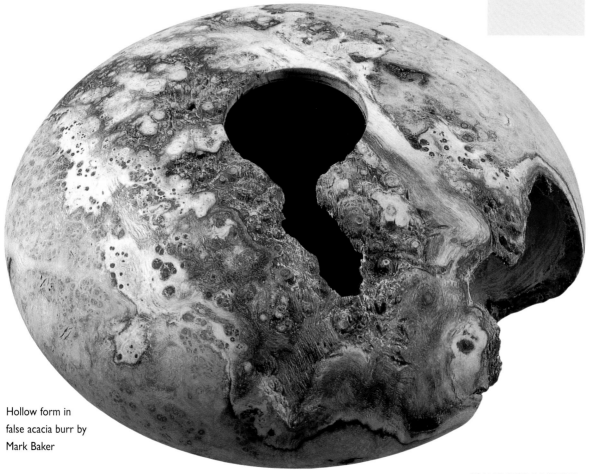

Hollow form in false acacia burr by Mark Baker

Redwood
Sequoia sempervirens

Other names
Californian redwood, coast redwood, sequoia. Burrs are sometimes sold as **vavona burr (burl)**

Burr, finished with acrylic lacquer

Grows
California and Oregon, USA
Height 200–325ft (60–100m)
Trunk diameter 10–15ft (3–4.6m), achieved during a lifespan of 800 years or more
Specific gravity .42
Typical dry weight 26lb/ft³ (420kg/m³)

Seasoning
Although the timber holds a lot of water when felled, it dries quickly and easily with hardly any degrade. It also shows minimal movement in use.
It can be wet-turned to completion and allowed to distort, or rough-turned and set aside to season fully before final turning.

Description

This is a true giant among softwoods – though it must not be confused with the giant redwood (*Sequoiadendron giganteum*). Massive sections of timber are available, allowing the turner a lot of scope to tackle almost any project imaginable: architectural, cabinetmaking, artistic or utilitarian. The sapwood is a near-white or pale whitish-yellow colour, and the heartwood ranges from a light red to a deep red-brown. This is not a very heavy or dense wood. It is straight-grained and has a texture ranging from fine to coarse, but is not capable of holding fine detail. The complementary earlywood and latewood form a clear growth-ring figure.

Burrs (burls) up to 6ft (1.8m) in diameter are fairly common, and are fantastically beautiful. They vary enormously in figuring, and will not disappoint anyone who wants to try them out. Be prepared to pay a high premium for them: they are highly sought-after by the cabinetmaking industry for veneers.

Working qualities

This is a lovely wood to work with. Wet timber cuts beautifully. Seasoned timber cuts well with sharp gouges and skew chisels, but shear-scraping is preferable to conventional scraping, to lessen the likelihood of grain tear-out or of leaving a woolly surface. A certain amount of dust is produced when turning seasoned wood, so be careful to exhaust it properly. Burrs can be a bit tricky, grain tear-out being the major problem; to minimize this, use sharp tools with a delicate, deliberate cut, avoid scraping and use abrasives to remove minor blemishes. This wood responds well to carving with both hand and power tools.

Abrasives can clog quickly when dry-sanding, especially if knots are present; knots may be quite resinous, but a fine finish can be achieved with either dry or wet sanding methods. Since the wood is very soft, take care not to sand too heavily in any one spot, but keep the abrasive moving all the time; failure to do this will result in hollows and surface depressions. Surface and penetrative finishes can be used to good effect to enhance the lovely grain pattern of this wood. However, the wood is quite 'hungry', so you may need quite a few coats to achieve a fine, even finish, especially on burrs.

Hollow form in redwood burr by Mark Baker

Hint

After turning, give the wood two or three coats of thinned-down sanding sealer, not allowing any of the coats to dry until the last one has been applied; then cut back with fine abrasive prior to applying wax or any other finish of your choice. This will seal the wood and provide a good foundation for any subsequent finish

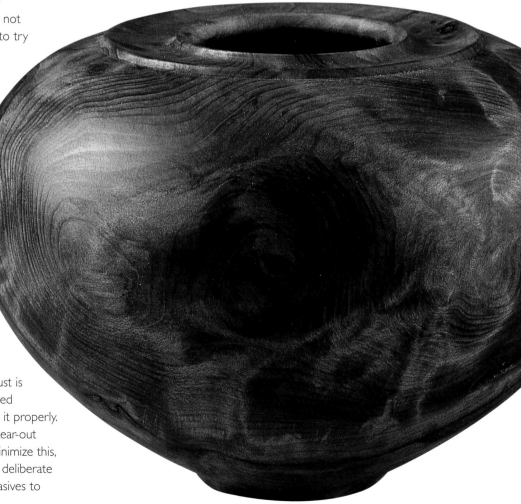

American mahogany

Swietenia macrophylla

Other names

Big-leaf mahogany, baywood, zopilote gateado, acahou, mogno, caoba, aguano; also Central American, Brazilian, Costa Rican etc. mahogany

Grows

Central America and northern parts of South America
Height 150ft (45m)
Diameter of trunk 6ft (1.8m)
Specific gravity .59
Dry weight 36lb/ft³ (590kg/m³)

Possible health risks

Dermatitis, respiratory problems, irritation, giddiness, vomiting, furunculosis

Seasoning

American mahogany dries easily; checking and distortion are minimal, and the seasoned wood is very stable. It responds well to rough-turning and setting aside to dry further before finish-turning.

Description

This highly lustrous wood varies a great deal in colour. It may be cream or yellowish, soft red, orange-pink or salmon-pink at first, maturing to a deep, rich red or brown. The grain may be straight, roey, curly or wavy. Irregular grain may produce very attractive figuring, including mottle, stripe or roe, blister and fiddleback patterns, but highly figured trees are usually snapped up by veneer manufacturers. It has a uniform texture which may be fine, medium or coarse. White deposits or dark gum may be visible in the pores.

Available in large sizes and highly prized in many woodworking disciplines, it is a valuable turning timber for architectural, cabinetmaking, utilitarian and artistic work.

Working qualities

The plain form of mahogany is a nice timber to work with, and will not present any problems to a turner who has mastered the basics of tool use. It cuts well with gouges and skews, producing long shavings and a fine finish straight off the tool. Scrapers can roughen the surface on end grain, and produce short shavings with some dust. Shear-scraping is a better option, but to my way of thinking a superior finish is produced from the gouge or skew, so try to get as good a cut as you can from those tools and then use abrasives to remove any minor blemishes. Figured pieces have irregular grain and are certainly better worked with gouges – followed by the skew chisel in the case of spindle work – to minimize grain tear-out. Scrapers would exacerbate the potential for tear-out. Mahogany carves well with power and hand tools, which adds another possible dimension for the turner.

It sands well with either dry or wet sanding methods, and readily accepts surface or penetrative finishes. It stains or dyes satisfactorily, but can be a little patchy if care is not taken to prepare the surface well; a wipe over with water or spirits (depending on the dyes being used) will help to even out the absorption rate of the dye.

Hint
If you want to adjust the colour of the wood a little – say, to a deeper red tint – consider colouring the finish before you apply it. This will result in a much more even coverage than some dyes and stains will produce. Oil can be tinted with artists' oil colour, or with the powdered or liquid dyes or tints used in the paint trade

Turned plaque
by John Hunnex

Yew

Taxus baccata

Other names
European yew,
yewtree

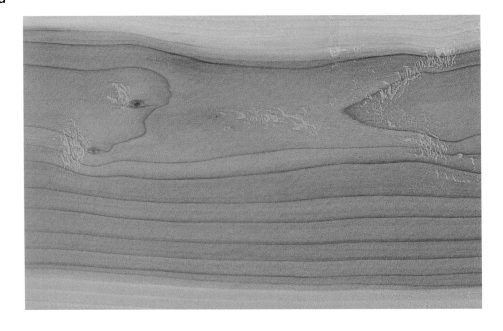

Grows

UK and mainland Europe, Turkey,
northern Iran, North Africa, the
Caucasus, the Himalayas and
Myanmar (Burma)

Height 50ft (15m)

Trunk diameter typically 1–3ft
(0.3–0.9m); old trees can be very
wide but tend to become hollow

Specific gravity .67

Typical dry weight 42lb/ft³
(670kg/m³)

Seasoning

This wood dries quickly and well, and
if care is taken there should be little
degrade. Slight distortion may occur,
and new shakes may form or existing
ones widen. The wood shows hardly
any movement in use. It is a lovely
wood to turn wet to completion. The
bark is thin, and can be retained in
the finished work: heart, sap and bark
make a truly stunning combination.
The movement in wet-turned pieces
varies considerably. The wood can
also be rough-turned and set aside
to season fully before finish-turning.

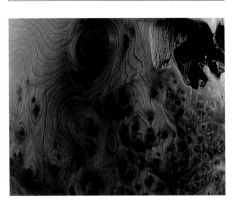

Burr (burl)

Description

The sapwood is a soft creamy-white and contrasts strongly with the darker heartwood, which ranges in colour from a golden orange-brown to a darker reddish-brown, and is commonly streaked with violet, red and purple. The wood will lose some of its fresh-cut vibrancy, mellowing to a darker orange-brown, but the darker streaking will always be present and distinct from the main body colour. There are frequently clusters of small knots and bark inclusions (pockets of ingrown bark). Although this medium-textured softwood is usually straight-grained, it can also be wavy, curly and irregular. Burrs are not uncommon, and can range from masses of tightly packed knots through to multicoloured, swirling grain. In short, you can never be truly sure what you will end up with until you start cutting. All of these features make it a truly exceptional wood, which is much sought-after for architectural, cabinetmaking, utilitarian and artistic work. Since the living tree is toxic, there is much debate as to whether the wood is safe to use for items that will come into contact with food. Some maintain that the choice of finish is important, but evidence is inconclusive.

Yew trees can live for over 1000 years. The wood is available in large sizes, affording considerable scope to the turner, but expect to find minute cracks or bark inclusions in larger pieces.

Working qualities

I love working with this wood: it has to be one of my all-time favourites. It cuts well most of the time, though irregular, sometimes interlocking grain can cause problems for skews and scrapers, resulting in grain tear-out. Be aware of this and choose your projects wisely, matching the wood to the project rather than trying to force it to do something that it is not suited for. If you experience tear-out with the skew chisel, change to a gouge and make very fine shearing cuts. I find that most turners are more confident with a gouge than a skew, so use the tools you feel happy with. Long ribbon shavings are produced when the wood is wet. Seasoned wood is more likely to produce small shavings with dust. The dust is very fine, with a peppery smell, so make sure that you can extract it as close to source as possible. The wood can be carved with both power and hand tools, but the former are recommended if irregular or interlocking grain is present.

Yew is prone to heat-checking, so be careful when sanding to use fresh, sharp abrasive. It sands well with both dry and wet methods. Use water or oil as a sanding lubricant (water for wet turning), but be careful to avoid colour contamination if there is sapwood present. Both penetrative and surface finishes can be used; my preference is for oil, which I power-buff to a fine, silky lustre.

Hollow form
by Mark Baker

Thuya

Tetraclinis articulata

Other names
Thuya burr,
thuyawood,
thyine wood,
citron burl,
sandarac tree

Burr (burl)

Grows
North Africa and southern Spain;
also east Africa, Cyprus and Malta
Height 50ft (15m)
Specific gravity .67
Typical dry weight 42lb/ft³
(670kg/m³)

Seasoning
The natural oil in the wood retards
moisture loss, which makes seasoning
easier. Kilning the wood slowly is
strongly recommended. Thuya can
either be wet-turned to completion,
or rough-turned, coated with PVA
and set aside to season further
before finish-turning.

! **Possible
health
risks**
Not known

Description

This softwood is spectacular to look at. The part of the tree that is used by woodturners is a root burr (burl) created by the repeated removal of the coppice growth, which stimulates increased growth underground. The burrs are a rich golden orange-brown or red-brown in colour, very knotty and contorted, with a fine, interlocked grain. The colour will darken over time to a mid-brown tone, losing its orange-red tint. The figuring is usually bird's-eye or mottled, and can be very attractive. This wood has a distinctive resinous or oily smell, which you will either love or hate. I do not like it, and unfortunately for me it is long-lasting.

Thuya burr is not available in very large sizes, and the rootstock is a highly irregular shape. It is mostly used for decorative veneers, carving, or other artistic work such as turning.

Working qualities

This resinous wood exudes an all-pervading smell when cut; I find this very 'heady' after a while, and it lingers for days. The contorted grain with lots of small knots means that grain tear-out is very likely. Skews are difficult to use on this wood, and gouges produce by far the best finish, but the resin is liable to build up on the bevel, which must be cleaned and sharpened frequently. Light, shallow cuts will minimize grain tear-out, but will not prevent it. A very light cut in conventional scraping mode can sometimes give a better finish than a gouge; shear-scraping works also. This is a wood that can be carved with both hand and power tools.

Abrasives clog readily with the resinous dust, but both dry and wet sanding methods produce a very fine finish, though checking can occur if too much heat is generated. Because of its oily nature, the wood can be resistant to surface finishes, so wipe it over with a solvent first to clear away the resin. It finishes well with oils and waxes, and can take a very high polish.

Box from Morocco, maker unknown

Hint
Because the wood is naturally resinous and oily, sand the work to completion and then power-buff using a polishing mop loaded with very fine abrasive held in a wax compound. This will produce a very fine lustre and, depending on the end use, may be the only finish that is needed

English elm

Ulmus procera

Other names
Elm, nave elm, red elm

Burr (burl)

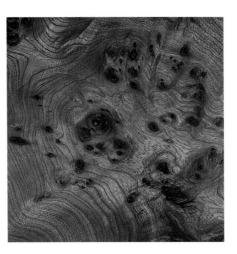

Grows
Northern Europe including UK
Height 80ft (24m)
Trunk diameter 3ft (0.9m)
Specific gravity .55
Typical dry weight 34lb/ft³ (550kg/m³)

Seasoning
The wood dries rapidly, with a strong likelihood of distortion unless closely stickered and weighted down, and can suffer from checks, splits and cell collapse. If you are rough-turning it before final seasoning, it may be wise to add an extra ¼in (6mm) or so of wall thickness per 12in (300mm) diameter to take into account the possible extra distortion, especially when using burrs. Alternatively, turn it to completion while wet, choosing a shape that will be enhanced by subsequent distortion, and leave it to move by itself.

Description

This is a wonderful timber both to look at and to work with. The heartwood is a soft tan to reddish-brown colour which is clearly distinct from the sapwood when freshly cut. The sapwood is not used. It will darken quite considerably on exposure, to a rich, deep reddish-brown colour. Elm is a medium to lightweight wood, somewhat coarse in texture, with prominent annual rings, and with a wonderful pattern of irregular and cross grain. The irregular growth rings, combined with the cross grain and speckled or feathery texture, result in an interesting figure. It is used for architectural, utilitarian and artistic work. It carves well.

It is available in large sections, giving the turner a lot of scope. It regularly forms burrs, which are highly prized by turners, veneer manufacturers and cabinetmakers alike, and command appropriately high prices. However, following the severe outbreak of Dutch elm disease in the 1970s, the supply of mature trees is now very limited.

Working qualities

Even though this wood has contorted and cross grain, it does not present many problems to the turner. Slow, deliberate cuts with sharp tools will be sufficient. There is a risk of end-grain tear-out, but this is not severe. Skew chisels can have a bit of trouble with the grain on spindle work. Gouges cut well. Scrapers used in conventional scraping mode may 'pull' the end grain or cross grain, but a light touch will help; shear-scraping is the better option.

Elm sands well by either dry or wet sanding methods, and readily accepts both surface and penetrative finishes. The grain, however, may need filling if an ultra-smooth finish is required. This can be achieved with either a proprietary grain filler, or a coat of sanding sealer followed by successive coats of a surface finish such as cellulose, cut back between coats.

Hint
Even if you use a surface finish such as lacquer or shellac (French polish), paste wax can be applied over it to create an even higher shine

Bowl in burr elm
by Mark Baker

Myrtle
Umbellularia californica

Other names
Acacia, baytree,
bay laurel,
California laurel,
mountain laurel,
Oregon myrtle,
pacific myrtle,
Californian
olive,
pepperwood,
spice tree

Figured sample

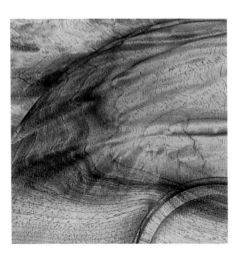

**Possible
health
risks**
Not known

Grows
Oregon and California, USA
Height 40–80ft (12–24m)
Trunk diameter 1ft 6in–2ft 6in
(0.5–0.8m)
Specific gravity .85
Typical dry weight 53lb/ft³
(850kg/m³)

Seasoning
Care must be taken when drying this
wood to avoid checking and warping.
It can be wet-turned to completion,
or rough-turned and set aside to dry
further. It is best to allow an extra
¼in (6mm) or so of wall thickness
per 12in (300mm) diameter when
rough-turning, to allow for the likely
degree of distortion. To minimize the
risk of checking, coat the end grain
or the whole of the rough-turned
piece with PVA adhesive to even out
the drying process.
   I gather the wood is sometimes
submerged in water to bring about
colour changes.

Description

This wonderful wood can be quite stunning when it has figuring in it. Even without figure, the wood itself is pleasant, with a subtle colour and grain pattern. The heartwood is a creamy, golden toffee-brown, often with a greenish tinge. The sapwood is a very similar colour and not easily distinguishable from the heartwood. The wood will darken considerably over time to a mid-brown tone. It is a dense, heavy wood whose grain – which is compact, smooth and close – is usually straight, but can be wavy or irregular. It frequently has ripple, feather, mottle or roe figuring. Myrtle is capable of holding fine detail, and is well worth considering if you want to make finial-topped boxes or other work that requires fine embellishment. It has a severe blunting effect on cutting edges, so frequent sharpening will be necessary.

It is a wood that can be used for utilitarian ware, artistic pieces, and architectural work such as balusters and chair legs. It is frequently used in cabinetmaking, so there is plenty of scope for making turned furniture parts. It is available in quite large sizes, giving turners ample opportunity to explore this wood with many different types of project.

Working qualities

This is a lovely wood to turn. It can, however, be a little tricky when the grain is irregular, especially when using a skew chisel on spindle work. Freshly sharpened gouges used with a light touch will minimize any tear-out. Shear-scraping is a better option than conventional scraping; both will fluff up the grain a little, but if light cuts are made the damage should be slight. I find it best to get as good a finish as I can from the gouge, then leave out the scraper stage and go straight to

abrasives to remove any minor ripples or blemishes. If the grain is straight, long ribbon shavings can be obtained from seasoned and wet wood alike. Very little dust is produced when cutting freshly seasoned wood, but old wood is a different matter. The dust is somewhat dirty and has an acrid, peppery smell to it. Myrtle can be carved with either hand or power tools.

It will sand well with either wet or dry sanding methods, but dry sanding will produce a lot of dust. Water, used as a sanding lubricant, will bleach the wood a little; oil, on the other hand, will add a nice warm glow to the work that can be enhanced by power buffing. Myrtle can be finished with both surface and penetrative finishes.

Hint

If you choose to power-sand large surfaces such as platters, use as large a sanding arbor as you can: 3, 4 or 5in (75, 100 or 125mm) if you can get them. These will make light work of the sanding process, smoothing out any ripples with ease

Bowl by Bert Marsh

> Even if you work with wood a lot, nature will always throw up amazing surprises

100 woods in brief

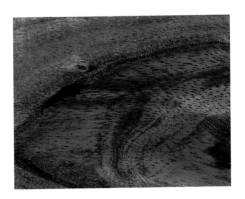

Koa

Acacia koa

Other names Black koa, curly koa, koaia, koa-ka, Hawaiian mahogany

Grows Hawaiian Islands

Height 80–100ft (24–30m)

Trunk diameter 3–4ft (0.9–1.2m)

Specific gravity .67

Typical dry weight 41lb/ft³ (670kg/m³)

Possible health risks Not known

Seasoning It dries easily with little or no degrade. There can be some surface checking on thicker stock. It is stable in use and retains its shape pretty well, even when turned to completion from partially seasoned stock. It can be wet-turned to completion, or rough-turned and set aside to season if you need to ensure minimal movement in items such as boxes.

Characteristics The uses of this very attractive wood include turning for furniture and joinery, utilitarian and decorative ware. The light brown sapwood is clearly distinct from the heartwood, which is mostly red-brown but can vary from pale cream through golden-brown to a deep reddish-chocolate colour. Koa yellows quickly in sunlight. The curly and wavy grain is moderately to strongly interlocked, which can produce beautiful fiddleback and roe figure. The growth rings show as black lines on longitudinal surfaces. Koa has a moderately coarse texture.

The wood cuts well with sharp gouges. Skew chisels cut well unless there is interlocking grain, which may tear out. Scrapers produce variable results, but usually give a surface that will require only a little abrading to remove blemishes. Shear-scraping may prove better on some surfaces than conventional scraping. If the wood is very dry, it may produce a fair amount of dust; this is much less likely with partially seasoned timber. It sands well, though with a risk of heat-checking, and finishes well. Oils darken the wood considerably, so try a lacquer coat instead to maintain the colour.

Australian blackwood

Acacia melanoxylon

Other names Black wattle

Grows Eastern Australia including Tasmania

Height Generally 33–80ft (10–24m) but can reach up to 115ft (35m)

Trunk diameter Generally 1ft 8in (0.5m) but can be up to 5ft (1.5m)

Specific gravity .66

Typical dry weight 41lb/ft³ (665kg/m³)

Possible health risks Dermatitis, asthma, nose and throat irritation

Seasoning Blackwood has relatively low shrinkage and remains moderately stable in service. It can be wet-turned to completion, or rough-turned and set aside to season before finish-tuning.

Characteristics The heartwood is generally golden-brown to darker brown, sometimes with a reddish tint and with dark brown, brown-black or reddish streaks. The sapwood is pale and up to 4in (100mm) wide. The grain is usually straight, with a medium, even texture, but sometimes interlocked, producing a fiddleback figure when quartersawn. Weight and hardness vary, the heavier timber generally coming from Tasmania. It blunts tool edges slightly. It takes fine detail and can be carved with hand or power tools. It is suitable for both decorative and utilitarian work.

This beautiful wood is a joy to turn, and will not present any problems to anyone who has mastered the basics of using tools. It sands well, but be careful of end-grain heat-checking, with either the dry or the wet sanding method. The latter should only be used if

there is no sapwood present. It receives surface and penetrative finishes reasonably well, and can be given a high polish. It has a naturally high lustre.

Figured

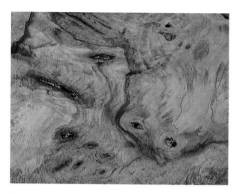

Buckeye

Aesculus spp.

Other names Stinking buckeye, fetid buckeye, Ohio buckeye, yellow buckeye

Grows USA: Pennsylvania to Nebraska, Alabama to Texas

Height 30–70ft (9–21m)

Trunk diameter 2ft (0.6m)

Specific gravity .47

Typical dry weight 29lb/ft³ (470kg/m³)

Possible health risks Not known

Seasoning This wood seasons easily with few cracking or checking problems. If it does split, it will not split straight, due to twisted grain. It can be turned wet, or partially or fully seasoned; but expect a lot of movement if it is not fully dry.

Characteristics Both heartwood and sapwood are almost white, with streaks of light to mid-grey and various blue-green tints. It is a strong, tough wood for its weight. The grain is straight or wavy, with fine texture and a high natural lustre. Ripple figuring may be revealed if the timber is cut radially. Available in quite large sizes, it is usually used for decorative or artistic work; it can be carved.

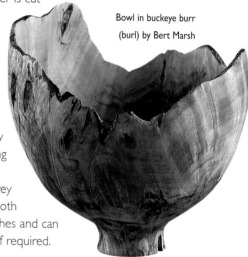

Bowl in buckeye burr (burl) by Bert Marsh

It is easy to work, though scrapers are likely to pluck out the grain, and it sands readily using the dry sanding method. Wet sanding would cause colour contamination in the non-grey areas. It will readily accept both surface and penetrative finishes and can be polished to a high gloss if required.

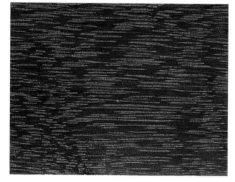

Afzelia

Afzelia spp.

Other names Doussié, apa, aligna, lingué, chamfuta, mkora, bolengo, m'banga, papao, uvala

Grows Tropical West Africa and East Africa

Height 80–100ft (25–30m)

Trunk diameter 4ft (1.2m)

Specific gravity .82

Typical dry weight 51lb/ft³ (820kg/m³)

Possible health risks Dermatitis, sneezing

Seasoning It can be kiln-dried slowly from green, with a risk of slight distortion, the extension of existing shakes and some fine checking. This is a wood best rough-turned and set aside to season fully.

Characteristics The orange or red-brown heartwood, which matures to a deep red-brown on exposure to air, is distinct from the pale straw-coloured sapwood. The grain of this dense, heavy wood is irregular and interlocked, giving a coarse yet even texture. Yellow or white deposits may cause staining. It is generally used for decorative turnery.

It is resistant to cutting with hand tools but turns well, although there is a risk of fluffing up the end grain (that is, creating a woolly surface) with scrapers, but with gouges and skews a fine finish can be achieved straight off the tool. It can be sanded with the wet (if no sapwood is present) or dry sanding methods, but is prone to heat-checking if excessive heat is generated. It will accept all finishes and can be taken to a high polish if the grain is filled.

Kauri pine

Agathis spp.

Other names New Zealand kauri
(*A. australis*), Queensland kauri (*A. robusta*,
A. palmerstonii, *A. microstachya*), East Indian kauri
(*A. dammara*) Fijian kauri (*A. vitiensis*)

Grows Australia, New Zealand, Papua New
Guinea, Philippines, Fiji, Indochina, Indonesia

Height 150ft (45m)

Trunk diameter 5–6ft (1.5–2m)

Specific gravity .48–.58

Typical dry weight 30–36lb/ft³
(480–560kg/m³)

Possible health risks Not known

Seasoning Dries reasonably well but can warp. Once seasoned, the wood is stable. It can be turned wet or partially seasoned to completion, but the finish off the tool can be woolly and require quite a lot of sanding; you must also expect some movement. Kiln-dried wood can be turned for furniture or joinery parts. When there is a need for precision, it responds well to rough-turning and setting aside to season.

Characteristics Kauri is deceptive: first impressions are that it is quite bland, but take a closer look and you can see subtle colour patterns that are very pretty. This lightweight softwood is useful for decorative and utilitarian turning. The heartwood varies from a creamy toffee colour, through darker pinkish-red hues to dark brown. It mellows quickly to a more uniform reddish-brown colour. Normally straight-grained with a fine, uniform texture, the wood can exhibit a streaked or mottled figure.

It cuts cleanly and easily with sharp bevel-rubbing tools and a slow traverse rate. It carves easily as well. Forget scrapers, which are likely to tear the grain – after gouges or skews, move straight to abrasives to remove blemishes. It sands well, as long as you do not skip grades. Oil darkens the wood a lot, and imparts an orange tinge; lacquer finishes with UV inhibitors darken less.

She-oak

Allocasuarina fraseriana (syn. *Casuarina fraseriana*) and related species

Other names Beefwood, Australian pine, horsetail tree, South-Sea ironwood, aru, ru, surra, agoho

Grows Australia, Africa, India, Indo-China, Philippines, Polynesia

Height 120–150ft (37–45m)

Trunk diameter 2ft–2ft 6in (0.6–0.76m)

Specific gravity .83

Typical dry weight 67lb/ft³ (1073kg/m³)

Possible health risks Not known

Seasoning It is difficult to dry and tends to warp and check; shrinkage can be high. This is a lovely wood for wet-turning to completion: subsequent movement creates some fantastic twisted forms. It can be rough-turned, allowing extra wall thickness to take account of the substantial shrinkage and distortion; coating the piece with PVA helps to avoid splitting.

Characteristics The heartwood ranges from pale orange-brown or red-brown to dark orange-brown or red-brown. The sapwood is a light buttery tan, quite different from the heartwood. The wood has a medium to fine texture, and shows distinct rays when cut radially. This is a hard, heavy, strong wood which can be used for utilitarian or decorative items.

It turns well, although it may splinter out at the edges of the work. There can be some pull-out on end grain, especially when scrapers are used; bevel-rubbing tools such as skews and gouges usually work better. It sands and finishes well.

Lace figure

American
or red alder

Alnus rubra

Other names Western alder, Oregon alder, Pacific coast alder

Grows Pacific coast of USA and Canada

Height 70–120ft (21–36m)

Trunk diameter 1–4ft (0.3–1.2m)

Specific gravity .53

Typical dry weight 33lb/ft³ (530kg/m³)

Possible health risks Dermatitis, rhinitis

Seasoning Red alder dries fairly rapidly and easily with almost no degrade. It moves very little once seasoned. It can be wet-turned to completion or rough-turned and set aside to dry prior to finish-turning.

Characteristics Red alder is a lightweight wood, fairly straight-grained, of uniform texture. The heartwood is pale yellow to reddish-brown, and the sapwood is not clearly differentiated. It has a pleasant but not outstanding visual appeal. This wood is suitable for utilitarian or artistic work, and can also be carved with hand or power tools.

It turns well, with few problems other than a slight risk of end-grain tear-out, especially when using a scraper in conventional scraping mode. Because it is soft, failure to keep the abrasive moving when sanding will cause hollows. Wet or dry sanding methods can be used. Red alder will accept both surface and penetrative finishes.

Curupay

Anadenanthera macrocarpa

Other names Not known

Grows Brazil

Height Medium

Trunk diameter 2–3ft (0.6–0.9m)

Specific gravity 1.05

Typical dry weight 66lb/ft³ (1050kg/m³)

Possible health risks Not known

Seasoning This wood dries slowly and is likely to split if dried in large sections. Rough-turn and set it aside to season before finish-turning.

Characteristics The heartwood is pale brown, but on exposure it turns red-brown with brown-black streaks. The sapwood is yellow to pinkish-brown. The grain is irregular and interlocked, and the wood has a fine, even texture. Because it is prone to splitting, through-cut boards are not commonly available; more often than not this wood is sold as air-dried, pre-dimensioned blanks from which artistic and decorative turning is created.

It turns and carves well, and holds fine detail. A very high polish can be obtained directly from bevel-rubbing tools (gouges or skew chisels). It can be sanded wet or dry, and can be taken to a fine finish with either penetrative or surface finishes. It is, however, prone to heat-checking.

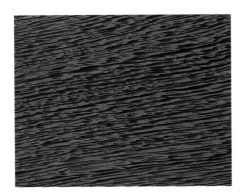

Red kabbas

Andira inermis

Other names Red cabbage bark, partridgewood, pheasantwood, angelin, angelim, andira, macaya, maquilla

Grows West Indies, Mexico, Central America, northern South America, Peru, Bolivia, Benin

Height 90–120ft (27–37m)

Trunk diameter 1ft 8in–2ft 4in (0.5–0.7m)

Specific gravity .64

Typical dry weight 40lb/ft³ (640kg/m³)

Possible health risks Not known

Seasoning It dries slowly, with a slight risk of checking and distortion. You are most likely to encounter partially seasoned wood in pre-dimensioned blanks, but occasionally boards may be available. If you turn it partially seasoned it will distort, which can be interesting. Rough-turning works well also.

Characteristics Red kabbas is a strong, tough, hard-wearing wood which is very interesting to look at. The pale sapwood is clearly demarcated from the pale yellow, mid-brown to deep red-brown heartwood. The heartwood also features lighter striping which, combined with the darker areas, resembles the pattern found on a partridge feather. It has a coarse texture and the grain is straight, but usually irregularly interlocked.

The wood cuts well, but when very dry it is somewhat dusty. It carves well. The best finish off the tool is achieved by using bevel-rubbing tools, though it also scrapes reasonably well despite its coarse texture. However, if care is not taken the wood is liable to fracture at the edges and where sharp detail is used. It sands and finishes well.

Paraná pine

Araucaria angustifolia

Other names Brazilian pine, pinheiro do Brasil, pino Paraná

Grows Brazil, Argentina, Paraguay

Height 80–100ft (24–33m)

Trunk diameter 5ft (1.5m)

Specific gravity .54

Typical dry weight varies widely, but approx. 33lb/ft³ (540kg/m³)

Possible health risks Not known

Seasoning This softwood, which is not a true pine, is difficult to season. The darker wood may distort, split and take a long time to dry. It shows moderate movement in service, but is prone to distortion if moisture conditions change. Kiln-dried stock can be turned for most projects, but when more stability is needed, rough-turn and treat the end grain with PVA to even out the drying process.

Characteristics The cream to soft brown heartwood has a darker inner core and may be streaked attractively with dark pink, red or red-brown. The grain is usually straight, and the wood has a close, uniform texture and faint growth rings. Small, tight knots may be present. It can be used for architectural work, balusters, spindles and so on; for utilitarian items such as pepper mills; and for artistic work. It can be carved as well. The irregular root nodules available from some suppliers are fun to turn and carve; they are dense and resinous.

This is an underrated wood that behaves more like a hardwood than a softwood. It works well with sharp bevel-rubbing tools (gouges and skews), but will suffer from grain tear-out if scrapers are used in conventional scraping mode. It sands well with wet or dry methods, and will accept any finish of your choice.

Norfolk Island pine

Araucaria cunninghamii

Other names Hoop pine, Australian araucaria, arakaria, Dorrigo pine, colonial pine

Grows Australia and Papua New Guinea

Height 100–150ft (30–45m) and above

Trunk diameter 2–4ft (0.6–1.2m) or more

Specific gravity .56

Typical dry weight 35lb/ft³ (560kg/m³)

Possible health risks Not known

Seasoning Norfolk Island pine dries quickly and well, without degrade. Take care to avoid blue stain, unless you like the effect; rapid but controlled drying will usually prevent it. The wood can be wet-turned to completion or rough-turned and set aside to dry.

Characteristics The heartwood can vary from white through to pale yellow-brown. The creamy-white sapwood, which is not clearly differentiated, is up to 6in (150mm) thick. The grain is straight, with a fine, uniform texture. This soft, light softwood is not a true pine.

It cuts well when wet, but if using seasoned timber you will need ultra-sharp tools; otherwise a woolly or torn surface is likely. Bevel-rubbing tools will give a better cut than scrapers, which can pluck out the grain. The wood can be sanded wet or dry, but care needs to be taken so as not to sand hollows and grooves. It can be finished with surface or penetrative finishes. A very high gloss can be achieved, but I find that a satin sheen shows off the wood to best effect.

Vase by Bert Marsh

Manzanita

Arctostaphylos spp.

Other names Not known

Grows Mexico; Oregon, Sierra Nevada mountains and California, USA

Height 27ft (8m)

Trunk diameter 4–10in (100–160mm)

Specific gravity .70

Typical dry weight 55lb/ft³ (881kg/m³)

Possible health risks Not known

Seasoning Severe splitting and checking are common during drying. Whether using the main trunk section or the root, rough-turning it and setting it aside to dry will not guarantee a split-free piece of wood. Wet-turning it to completion, with a thin, uniform wall thickness, is a better option, but the inevitable distortion means that boxes with tight-fitting lids, for example, could not be undertaken. If this is what you want to make, try rough-turning, then coating the whole piece in PVA before setting it aside to dry.

Characteristics The heartwood is red-brown to red, and the narrow sapwood is light brown. There is often attractive figure and grain. This is a hard, strong wood with a fine texture.

It is easy to turn, producing a fine polish from bevel-rubbing tools as well as scrapers. It sands well with both wet (if sapwood is not present) and dry methods, and can be brought to a high polish.

The root sections which are available in all different shapes and sizes are usually a deep red-brown or maroon colour, and sometimes display a very dramatic swirling figure. These are highly prized by carvers, who can make good use of the contorted, twisted forms. Turners, however, need to find larger sections which they can dimension as necessary. I find it best to wet-turn the root sections to completion, but even so I have had a high failure rate.

Peroba rosa

Aspidosperma peroba

Other names Rosa peroba, red peroba, palo rosa, amarello, amargosa, ibri romi

Grows Argentina and Brazil

Height 90ft (27m)

Trunk diameter 2ft 6in (0.75m) or more

Specific gravity .75

Typical dry weight 47lb/ft³ (750kg/m³)

Possible health risks Skin irritation, headache, sweating, respiratory problems, nausea, stomach cramps, fainting, drowsiness, weakness and blisters

Seasoning This is a fast-drying wood with a high shrinkage rate, so care needs to be taken to reduce the risk of splitting and distortion. You can wet-turn the work to completion, or use partially seasoned stock, but you must expect some movement. For minimal movement, rough-turn and set it aside to season before finish-turning. When rough-turning, allow an extra ¼in (6mm) or so of wall thickness per 12in (300mm) diameter to allow for the high shrinkage rate.

Characteristics The heartwood varies greatly in colour, but is generally pinkish- or reddish-brown, with purple, orange or yellow streaks, but darkens on exposure. The yellow sapwood is not very distinct from the heartwood. The grain may be straight or irregular, with a fine or very fine texture and a low to medium lustre. This hard, heavy timber has a moderate blunting effect on edge tools, but holds fine detail.

It turns well with sharp tools, sands and finishes well, and will not present any problems other than the risk of heat-checking in end grain, and the high shrinkage rate of the wet wood.

Pau marfim

Balfourodendron riedelianum

Other names Marfim, gutambu, pau liso, moroti, kyrandy, ivorywood

Grows Argentina, Brazil, Paraguay

Height 40–80ft (12–24m)

Trunk diameter 1–4ft (0.3–1.2m)

Specific gravity .80

Typical dry weight 50lb/ft³ (800kg/m³)

Possible health risks Dermatitis, rhinitis and asthma

Seasoning This wood dries easily with little degrade. There is only small movement in service. Rough-turning is recommended, after which it should be coated with PVA to even out the drying rate.

Characteristics Both heartwood and sapwood look much the same, the colour ranging from almost white to pale yellow-brown or off-white to creamy-yellow. Sometimes there is a hint of grey, and darker streaks. The grain may be straight or irregular, and can be interlocked. The texture is fine and the wood has a medium lustre. This is a very hard, dense wood, and has a moderate to severe blunting effect on tool edges. It can be carved, and is available in reasonably large sizes, but the cost can be high, so it is more frequently used for smaller decorative items.

This wood is a delight to work with, as long as it is straight-grained: it cuts well with all tools, but frequent sharpening will be necessary. When the grain is irregular, tear-out is likely. It sands satisfactorily, but is prone to heat-check on the end grain. Wet or dry sanding methods can be used. It polishes well; if required, a highly polished finish is possible.

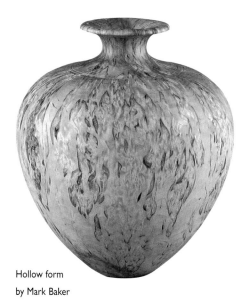

Hollow form

by Mark Baker

Masur birch
Betula alba

Other names European birch; English, Finnish, Swedish birch

Grows Northern and eastern Europe

Height 40–65ft (12–20m)

Trunk diameter 1ft 2in (0.35m)

Specific gravity .67

Typical dry weight 42lb/ft³ (670kg/m³)

Possible health risks Dermatitis and respiratory problems

Seasoning It dries quickly with high risk of end splitting. Shrinkage is quite high, but once dry, the wood is stable. It is prone to fungal growth if left freshly sawn for long before drying. It can be wet-turned to completion, or rough-turned and set aside to season before finish-turning.

Characteristics *Betula alba*'s heartwood and sapwood are similar, both being creamy-white to pale brown in colour. There may also be subtle silvering and darkening. This wood can display a flecked, flame-like figuring, caused by beetle larvae attacking the cambium, which is very attractive, and the name **masur** is given to logs which show this figuring. The wood can also have interlocking grain, which exhibits a ripple of curly figure when cut.

The wood is easy to turn wet or seasoned, but the grain can fluff up a little. When working seasoned wood, small shavings are produced with some dust. It sands well with either wet or dry sanding methods, but since it is soft, take care not to sand hollows in the wood. It can be finished with either penetrative or surface finishes.

American yellow birch
Betula alleghaniensis

Other names Hard birch, Canadian yellow birch, Quebec birch, swamp birch, betula wood

Grows Eastern Canada and eastern USA

Height 70–100ft (21–30m)

Trunk diameter 2ft 6in (0.8m)

Specific gravity .71

Typical dry weight 44lb/ft³ (710kg/m³)

Possible health risks Dermatitis and respiratory problems

Seasoning It dries slowly with little degrade, but shrinkage can be high, which may result in end and surface checks. Honeycombing and collapse can occur in wet heartwood. There is a considerable movement in use, so dimensional stability is poor. It is advisable to rough-turn the work, allowing an extra ⅜in (10mm) of wall thickness per 12in (300mm) diameter, before setting it aside to season. Alternatively, wet-turn the piece to completion. Use kiln-dried wood for turning furniture or joinery parts.

Characteristics The sapwood is whitish, pale yellow or light red-brown, the heartwood red-brown, but colours may vary. Yellow birch has a fine, even texture and a mostly straight, close grain. Wavy and curly grain can occur, and such pieces are prized for their pleasing figure.

Sharp bevel-rubbing tools will give the best finish; scrapers will damage the surface. Careful sanding will produce a very fine finish, but keep the abrasive moving or you will sand away the soft areas, leaving the harder parts proud. Both penetrative and surface finishes will yield good results. This wood can also be stained or dyed.

Muhuhu

Brachylaena hutchinsii

Other names Mkarambaki, muhugive, muhugwe

Grows East Africa

Height 80–90ft (24–27m)

Trunk diameter 2ft (0.6m)

Specific gravity .93

Typical dry weight 58lb/ft³ (930kg/m³)

Possible health risks Dermatitis

Seasoning This dense wood needs to be dried slowly to minimize degrade. It has a tendency towards end splitting and surface checking. Partially seasoned stock can be turned to completion, but will move a little. I prefer rough-turning and coating the piece with PVA before seasoning further.

Characteristics The heartwood is a mid-tan colour when freshly cut, then mellows to a darker chestnut-brown, often with dark streaks and a green tinge. The grain is closely interlocked, sometimes wavy or curly, with a fine, even texture. The sapwood is quite distinct, being grey-white. This is an aromatic wood, with a scent similar to sandalwood.

Usually only small sections are available, typically pre-dimensioned blanks rather than logs. It cuts satisfactorily, and a fine finish is achievable with most tools, but it is prone to splintering off at the edges. It will also heat-check if excessive heat is generated during sanding. It sands well and is receptive to both surface and penetrative finishes.

Satiné bloodwood

Brosimum paraense

Other names Not known

Grows Brazil

Height Small to medium-sized tree

Trunk diameter 1ft 8in (0.5m)

Specific gravity 1.15

Typical dry weight 71lb/ft³ (1150kg/m³)

Possible health risks Not known

Seasoning It dries slowly and is very likely to split and check, but is very stable when dry. Partially seasoned wood can be turned, but will move. It can also be rough-turned and set aside to season more fully before finish-turning.

Characteristics The heartwood ranges from grey-red to deep red, often with yellow and red stripes. The grain is straight or interlocked, with a very fine texture. It is not available in large sizes, so decorative and artistic work is usually undertaken with this wood.

The wood is very hard and blunts tool edges severely. It is easier to turn than to machine, but may contain silica, which will blunt tools rapidly. It cuts quite well with all sharp tools, especially with bevel-rubbing tools. It sands well, although the abrasive clogs readily and there is a risk of heat-checking on the end grain. A better surface finish is created by wet sanding. It can be brought to a high-gloss finish with either penetrative or surface finishes.

Verawood

Bulnesia arborea

Other names Guayacán, Maracaibo lignum vitae

Grows Colombia and Venezuela

Height 40–50ft (12–15m)

Trunk diameter 2ft (0.6m)

Specific gravity 1.0

Typical dry weight 62lb/ft³ (1000kg/m³)

Possible health risks Not known

Seasoning This oily, resinous wood dries slowly; large sections never dry thoroughly. It can be turned part-seasoned or wet, but expect some movement or surface checking. Rough-turning and setting aside to season is usually successful: small surface checks can be removed during final turning, or filled with PVA and dust.

Characteristics Verawood self-lubricates like lignum vitae (*Guaiacum officinale*), and has similar applications. It is not quite so heavy as lignum vitae, but prettier and easier to work. It is dense, hard, strong and abrasion-resistant. The heartwood varies from a soft green-brown to a brighter green, often with attractive streaks of darker greenish-brown. The colour lasts well. The fine, sometimes interlocked grain holds fine detail and hand-chased threads well. It gives off a pleasant smell when worked.

Scrapers may produce a finer finish than gouges or skews – bevel-rubbing tools tend to gum up quickly, which makes them skip over the surface. In either case the wood produces some oily dust. Abrasives need frequent cleaning, but after careful toolwork only minimal sanding should be necessary. It resists penetrative finishes, but oils and waxes can be used effectively to polish the wood. Surface finishes may lift off or fail to take; wiping over with solvent may help. If you use a power-buffing mop, loaded with a fine abrasive held in a wax compound, to polish the surface, the natural oils and resins themselves make a fine finish. Be careful not to generate too much heat – there is a risk of heat-checking.

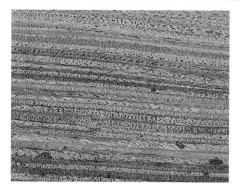

Palo santo

Bulnesia sarmienti

Other names Argentine lignum vitae. Botanical name variously given as *B. sarmienti* or *B. sarmientoi*

Grows Paraguay and Argentina

Height 30ft (9m)

Trunk diameter 1ft–1ft 4in (0.3–0.4m)

Specific gravity 1.1

Typical dry weight 69lb/ft³ (1100kg/m³)

Possible health risks Not known

Seasoning This wood dries very slowly and is prone to checking. Rough-turning the piece then coating it with PVA before setting it aside to dry is recommended. Conversely it can be turned to completion, with an even wall thickness, from partially seasoned stock, but in this case it will move a bit.

Characteristics The heartwood is olive-green to brown with variegated stripes, mellowing quickly to a rich greenish-brown. It is oily to the touch, and fragrant. The sapwood is a narrow strip of off-white wood. Palo santo has a fine, even texture and an interwoven grain.

It is difficult to machine but easier to turn. It polishes well, but is resistant to some penetrative and surface finishes. Often sold as a substitute for lignum vitae (*Guaiacum officinale*), it has many of the same characteristics: it turns and finishes in the same way, has a similar smell, but is not quite as dense – although it will take a hand-chased thread. Abrasives are liable to clog, but if there is no sapwood present, wet sanding will produce a very fine finish; wipe over to remove any residual slurry before applying a final coat of finish.

Pernambuco

Caesalpinia echinata, syn.
Guilandina echinata

Other names Brazilwood, Bahia wood, Para wood, pau Brasil, Brazil ironwood, brasilete

Grows Eastern Brazil

Height 25–40ft (8–12m)

Trunk diameter 1ft 8in–2ft 3in (0.5–0.7m)

Specific gravity 1.2

Typical dry weight 75–80lb/ft³ (1200–1280kg/m³)

Possible health risks Irritation to eyes and skin, headaches, nausea, visual disturbance

Seasoning This wood is expensive, so dry it very slowly to avoid degradation and checking. I recommend rough-turning it and leaving it to season before finish-turning; this will give maximum stability. It can be turned to completion from partially seasoned stock, but is likely to distort a bit.

Characteristics The heartwood is bright orange-red, maturing to a deep red-brown. The sapwood is almost white. There can be a stripy or marbled figure, sometimes with pin knots. The grain may be straight or interlocked, with a fine, even texture and a natural lustre. The wood is mostly used for artistic or decorative work.

This hard, heavy wood blunts tool edges severely, but turns surprisingly well, with very few problems – end-grain heat-checking being the worst of these. A fine finish can be achieved straight from the tool. It sands well with any method, and can be polished to a wonderful lustrous finish with either penetrative or surface finishes.

Guayacán partridgewood

Caesalpinia paraguariensis, syn.
C. melanocarpa, Acacia paraguariensis

Other names Guayacán

Grows Paraguay

Height up to 1ft 4in (0.4m)

Trunk diameter Not known

Specific gravity 1.25

Typical dry weight 78lb/ft³ (1250kg/m³)

Possible health risks Not known

Seasoning Dries slowly and tends to have surface checks if dried in larger sections. I recommend rough-turning it and setting it aside to dry before finish-turning.

Characteristics This is a wonderful-looking wood. The heartwood is dark olive-brown or yellow-brown with dark brown or black lines; plainsawn surfaces have a figure reminiscent of partridge feathers. The narrow sapwood is yellow-white. The grain is straight to interlocked with a very fine, even texture. The samples I have are of a slightly oily nature, though this wood is not generally described as oily. It is not available in large sizes, so is usually reserved for artistic or decorative work.

It is very dense, hard, and capable of holding very fine detail. It turns well with freshly sharpened tools. Abrasives tend to clog when sanding, and care is needed to avoid heat-checking. If no sapwood is present it can be sanded wet rather than dry. It can be finished to a high polish with either penetrative or surface finishes.

Genero lemonwood

Calycophyllum multiflorum

Other names Not known

Grows Central and South America

Height Small to medium tree

Trunk diameter Not known

Specific gravity .82–.86

Typical dry weight 51–54lb/ft³ (820–860kg/m³)

Possible health risks Not known

Seasoning It dries rapidly with only slight end-checking. It can be turned wet or partially seasoned, though subsequent movement is erratic. If stability is required, rough-turn it and then set it aside to season before finish-turning.

Characteristics The heartwood is a creamy yellow-brown, with slightly lighter cream-coloured sapwood. The grain is straight or slightly interlocked, with a fine, even texture. It is capable of holding fine detail and can be carved with hand or power tools. It is not available in very large sections; usually it is sold as air-dried, pre-dimensioned blanks and is used for small decorative or artistic work.

It turns, sands and finishes well, although it is prone to heat-checking on end grain. It is often used as an alternative to European boxwood (*Buxus sempervirens*), because it works similarly and is not too dissimilar in looks, whether fresh-cut or aged; but it is not as dense as box, and will not hold hand-chased threads. It is available in larger sizes than boxwood.

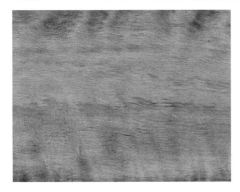

European hornbeam

Carpinus betulus

Other names Not known

Grows Europe, Turkey, Iran

Height 50–80ft (15–24m)

Trunk diameter 3–4ft (0.9–1.2m)

Specific gravity .75

Typical dry weight 47lb/ft³ (750kg/m³)

Possible health risks Not known

Seasoning Hornbeam dries easily, with little degrade. It can be wet-turned to completion, worked partially seasoned, or rough-turned and seasoned before finish-turning, depending on your choice of project.

Characteristics This wood has a pleasant, subtle figure and colour variation. It is quite dense and hard-wearing. The heartwood and sapwood look much alike: both are a dull creamy-white or milky colour, with occasional yellow-green streaking. Crossed or irregular grain is the norm, and it has a fine, even texture. Quartersawn surfaces may have a flecked appearance, produced by the broad medullary rays. It can also exhibit a mottled figure. It holds fine detail and is a good wood to use both for utilitarian and for decorative or artistic work.

Hornbeam turns quite well, though end-grain tear-out is a possibility when scrapers are used, whether in conventional or shear-scraping mode. Sanding is satisfactory with wet or dry methods, and the wood readily accepts both surface and penetrative finishes.

Hickory

Carya spp., syn. *Hicoria* spp.

Other names Pignut hickory (*C. glabra*), mockernut hickory (*C. tomentosa*), shellbark hickory (*C. laciniosa*), shagbark hickory, scalybark hickory (*C. ovata*)

Grows Canada and USA

Height 50–100ft (15–30m)

Trunk diameter 2ft 6in (0.8m)

Specific gravity .82

Typical dry weight 51lb/ft³ (820kg/m³)

Possible health risks Not known

Seasoning It dries quickly, and this requires careful management: shrinkage, twisting and warping can be major problems if drying is too rapid. The wood can be wet-turned to completion and allowed to distort, or rough-turned and set aside to season before finish-turning. You might consider allowing an extra ¼in (6mm) of wall thickness per 12in (300mm) diameter to allow for the likely shrinkage and twisting. Kiln-dried wood is fine for utilitarian and joinery work.

Characteristics There is little difference between the four species of hickory available commercially. The sapwood, which is pale and clearly distinct from the heartwood, is sold as **white hickory**. The heartwood is a mid-brown to red-brown, and sold as **red hickory**. The grain is usually straight but can be irregular or wavy, with quite a coarse texture.

It has a marked blunting effect on cutting edges, so tools will have to be sharpened regularly. It is satisfactory to turn, but the best finish is with bevel-rubbing tools. It can be carved. It is easy to sand and accepts finishes well. It is commonly used for furniture, joinery and utilitarian work, and for items requiring high impact resistance.

Pecan

Carya illinoiensis

Other names Pecan nut

Grows Canada and USA

Height 160ft (50m)

Trunk diameter 6ft (1.8m)

Specific gravity .61

Typical dry weight 55lb/ft³ (881kg/m³)

Possible health risks Not known

Seasoning Pecan kiln-dries well, and air-dries fairly rapidly. There is moderate shrinkage, and twisting and warping can be a problem, especially when air-drying.

Characteristics Pecan is available in large sizes, suitable for a wide range of projects, but it is noted chiefly for its strength and is commonly used where durability and high impact resistance are required: furniture, handles, flooring and so on. It can also be used for decorative and utilitarian turning. It is a pleasant wood to turn. The sapwood is a very light cream colour and the heartwood is a soft, mid-toned brown to pinkish-red, tinged with brown. The wood has a medium texture and can be somewhat brittle, so be careful of sharp edges or very fine detail.

It cuts well with sharp bevel-rubbing tools, but scrapers, if not used sensitively, are liable to pluck or rough up the surface, especially on end grain. My favoured method is to use bevel-rubbing tools and then go straight to abrasives to remove minor blemishes. It will accept penetrative or surface finishes.

Blackbean

Castanospermum australe

Other names Beantree, Moreton Bay bean, Moreton Bay chestnut

Grows Eastern Australia

Height 120ft (37m)

Trunk diameter 3–4ft (1.0–1.2m)

Specific gravity .70

Typical dry weight 44lb/ft³ (700kg/m³)

Possible health risks Dermatitis; irritation to nose, eyes, throat, armpits and genitals

Seasoning This wood is difficult to dry. To reduce the risk of honeycombing and cell collapse, air-dry first, then kiln-dry for more control. If turning wet or partially seasoned wood, expect some movement. For joinery or furniture parts, kiln-dried stock is fine. To minimize movement, rough-turn and set aside to season, coating with PVA to guard against surface checking.

Characteristics This handsome wood is hard and heavy. It is somewhat oily, and can be brittle. The heartwood is a mid-chocolate to reddish-chocolate colour; darker streaks may be deep reddish-brown or black-brown. The sapwood is creamy-white or yellowish. The wood darkens considerably with age. The texture is medium to coarse, the grain usually straight but sometimes interlocked. Quartersawn wood may be attractively striped. The wood is valued by cabinetmakers, and turners can use it for decorative, artistic or utilitarian work. It can also be carved.

It cuts cleanly in most instances. Bevel-rubbing tools leave a reasonable finish. Scrapers do not cut so well, and the surface will need some sanding; end-grain tear-out is likely if interlocking grain is present. Keep tools sharp and make slow, deliberate cuts. Be careful when turning beads, or near the edges of work: it can splinter or break out. Oily, sticky dust is produced during turning. The wood sands acceptably, but abrasives clog quickly. There is a risk of heat-checking on the end grain. Both penetrative and surface finishes can be used, but grain-filling may be needed.

American hackberry

Celtis occidentalis

Other names Common hackberry, bastard elm, sugarberry, nettletree, hoop ash

Grows Canada and eastern USA

Height 80ft (25m)

Trunk diameter 1ft 6in–3ft (0.5–0.9m), sometimes more

Specific gravity .64

Typical dry weight 40lb/ft³ (640kg/m³)

Possible health risks Not known

Seasoning Hackberry dries readily with minimal degrade, but there is a risk of buckling because of curvature in the trunk. It exhibits fairly high shrinkage and may move in use.

Characteristics Hackberry is a member of the elm family, and closely related to sugarberry (*C. laevigata*). The sapwood, which is very wide and makes up most of the timber content of the tree, is yellow-grey or green-grey to light brown. The small area of heartwood, if present, is a greenish yellow-grey to soft grey-brown, sometimes with lighter streaks of greenish-yellow. The wood is susceptible to blue staining and has irregular grain, sometimes straight and sometimes interlocked, with a fine, uniform texture. It is capable of holding fine detail. It is used for functional and utilitarian work, furniture and decorative turnings.

Once seasoned, it cuts well with bevel-rubbing tools – less well with scrapers, but any blemishes are easily removed with abrasive. It sands well using dry or wet methods, and accepts finishes and stains readily.

Greenheart

Chlorocardium rodiaei, syn. *Ocotea rodiaei*, *Nectandra rodiaei* (also *rodiei*)

Other names Demerara, viruviru; yellow, brown, black, white greenheart

Grows Guyana, Surinam, Brazil, Venezuela, some Caribbean islands

Height 75–125ft (23–38m)

Trunk diameter 3ft (0.9m)

Specific gravity 1.03

Typical dry weight 64lb/ft³ (1030kg/m³)

Possible health risks Cardiac and intestinal disorders, throat irritation; splinters are toxic

Seasoning Greenheart dries slowly and degrade can be considerable, especially in thick wood, with end-splitting, checking and lengthening of existing shakes.

Characteristics This is a dense, hard, very heavy wood. The heartwood can range from a light yellow-green, through dark green with tinges of brown or yellowish-brown, to dark brown or black; it may have some dark streaking as well. The grain is straight to roey, sometimes interlocked, with a fine, uniform texture. It is capable of holding fine detail. The sapwood, which looks similar to the heartwood, is pale greenish-yellow.

Interlocking grain makes this a tricky wood to work with. Bevel-rubbing tools are the best option to achieve a reasonable finish off the tool; then go straight to abrasives to remove any minor blemishes. Scrapers will result in a lot of tear-out, even if used in shear-scraping mode. Whichever tools are used, there is a tendency for sharp edges to break away, flake or splinter. Abrasives will clog quickly, but a fine finish can be achieved. Greenheart resists some surface finishes; penetrative finishes such as oil do not penetrate far, but do polish up nicely. Be careful of splinters, which turn septic very quickly; the dust can also have unpleasant effects.

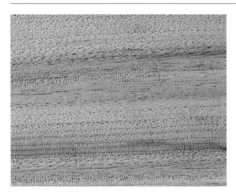

Camphor or camphor laurel

Cinnamomum camphora

Other names Camphor-tree, kusonoki, ohez, kalingag, dalchini, kayu

Grows Japan, Taiwan, China, Australia; cultivated in southern USA

Height 60–100ft (18–30m) or more

Trunk diameter 2–4ft (0.6–1.2m)

Specific gravity .35–.50

Typical dry weight 26–38lb/ft³ (416–609kg/m³)

Possible health risks Not known

Seasoning Air-dries well, with some shrinkage, occasionally with slight warping. The wood is stable once dried.

Characteristics This tree is classified as a weed in Australia; it is so invasive that there is large-scale clearance under way to give native timbers a chance to grow. The lightweight wood has a medium to fine texture. The heartwood and sapwood are both light creamy-tan to light tan, with darker streaks of greenish-pink, red or brown. The grain is usually straight but sometimes interlocked or wavy, with a high natural lustre. It sometimes shows mottled or roe figure. Large sizes are available, so many types of project are possible.

This is a soft, light wood, easy to work; it sands and finishes well and can be taken to a silky-smooth finish with a high lustre. The wood has a distinctive smell – clothes boxes used to be made from this wood to keep moths out. I find the smell pleasant, but it fades with time – as does the colour.

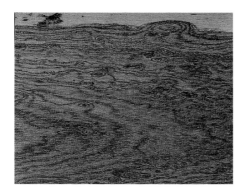

Bocote

Cordia gerascanthus, C. elaeagnoides

Other names Mexican rosewood, grand palisander, lauro pardo, lauro negro, Ecuador laurel, princewood, Spanish elm, anacanuite

Grows Mexico

Height 70–100ft (21–30m)

Trunk diameter Not known

Specific gravity .85 but varies widely

Typical dry weight 53lb/ft³ (850kg/m³)

Possible health risks Not known

Seasoning This is a difficult wood to season: surface checking and end-splitting are common. It can be wet-turned but, because it is only available in sizes suitable for small to medium-sized decorative turnings, it is more commonly turned to completion from partially seasoned stock, or rough-turned and then set aside to season. Coating it with PVA after rough-turning will even out the drying process and reduce the likelihood of splitting.

Characteristics This is a reasonably dense, oily wood with a medium to fine texture. It has a very attractive appearance. The heartwood ranges from a soft, mid-toned red-brown to a deep brown with deep reddish-brown to black streaks. The sapwood is a pale creamy-white tinged with grey. It is capable of holding quite fine detail.

It cuts very well with bevel-rubbing tools, but only tolerably well with scrapers, even in shear-scraping mode. Some dust is produced during the cut; this is sticky and clinging, with a strong but not unpleasant smell. The wood sands satisfactorily, but will heat-check if you are not careful. It can be taken to a high polish with either surface or penetrative finishes.

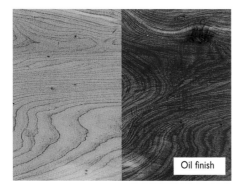

Oil finish

Cypress

Cupressus spp.

Other names Mexican cypress

Grows Southern and central USA, South America, southern and eastern Africa, Australia, New Zealand

Height 70–100ft (21–30m)

Trunk diameter 3ft (1m)

Specific gravity .48

Typical dry weight 30lb/ft³ (480kg/m³)

Possible health risks Not known

Seasoning Cypress dries quickly but does not degrade much. For furniture, or for architectural work such as balusters and spindles – the commonest use for this wood – you can use kiln-dried stock that has been acclimatized in the workshop for a bit. For decorative or artistic work, it can either be wet-turned to completion, using a thin, even wall thickness, or rough-turned and set aside to season before finish-turning.

Characteristics This is a soft, lightweight softwood. The heartwood is pale creamy-yellow to pinkish-brown, the sapwood a bit lighter. There are sometimes streaks of resin. The grain is quite straight, with a fine, even texture; cultivated trees may have more knots.

The wood is satisfactory to work with freshly honed bevel-rubbing tools, but does not finish well from the scraper. It is best to go straight from chisel or gouge to using abrasives. Cypress can be a bit brittle, so do not leave sharp edges which may break out. Knots are prone to tear-out. Sanding is OK, but the abrasive may clog. Because the wood is soft, care has to be taken, especially with power sanding, not to concentrate on one place too much, or hollows will be created. Cypress takes penetrative or surface finishes well.

This comparatively inexpensive wood is excellent to practise on. You can see immediately if the tools are sharp and the cutting approach angle is correct – if not, the grain will tear out.

Rimu

Dacrydium cupressinum

Other names Red pine

Grows New Zealand (supply is strictly regulated by legislation)

Height 80–100ft (24–30m)

Trunk diameter 6ft 6in (2m)

Specific gravity .53

Typical dry weight 33lb/ft³ (530kg/m³)

Possible health risks Dust may irritate eyes and nose

Seasoning Rimu kiln-dries and air-dries reasonably well, but may surface-check. Joinery or furniture parts can be turned to completion from kiln-dried stock. Rimu can be rough-turned and set aside to season further, but the movement is so small that I have found no need to do this except for precision items such as lidded boxes. If the wood is very wet, expect movement; you can either turn it wet to completion with a thin wall thickness, or rough-turn it and set it aside to season.

Characteristics The wood is a medium yellowish-tan or reddish-tan, sometimes with an orange-yellow tint. It has irregular darker streaks which fade a lot on exposure to light. The wood is straight-grained with a fine, even, uniform texture. The heartwood can exhibit an attractive figure, caused by various-coloured pigments in the wood; these are liable to fade, but will remain vibrant for longer if you use a finish that contains UV inhibitors.

This is a lovely wood to work, whether turning or carving. It cuts very well with skews and gouges, leaving a silky-smooth surface straight off the tool. Scrapers, however, are likely to tear out the end grain; a very delicate shear-scraping cut is slightly better, but not much. After profiling with bevel-rubbing tools, go straight to abrasive to remove any blemishes. Rimu sands well and readily accepts both surface and penetrative finishes. It can, however, be a little finish-hungry, so a few coats may be necessary to ensure even coverage.

Brazilian kingwood

Dalbergia cearensis

Other names Violete, violetta, violet wood

Grows South America, mostly Brazil

Height 50–100ft (15–30m)

Trunk diameter 4–8in (100–200mm)

Specific gravity 1.2

Typical dry weight 75lb/ft³ (1200kg/m³)

Possible health risks Eye and skin irritation

Seasoning It can split when being air-dried, I find, but kiln-dries well with little degrade. It is a wood best rough-turned and set aside to season before finish-turning; you can coat the piece with PVA if you wish. Partially seasoned pieces can be turned, but unless they are turned thin they are likely to check; there will be some movement.

Characteristics This stunning timber shows a variety of colours in the heartwood. The basic colour is a rich purple-brown, but parts may be almost black or purplish-black, with streaks of deep, rich violet red, rich violet-brown and black, and occasionally a creamy-red tinged with yellow. It is quite oily, with a fine, uniform texture that holds detail well. The creamy-white sapwood contrasts starkly with the heartwood; it is usually removed before the wood is exported, but when present it can be used to good visual effect. It is an expensive wood, and veneer companies and cabinetmakers tend to snaffle large quantities of it. It is only available in small sizes, either as pre-dimensioned blanks or as sections of trunk, so small or medium-sized decorative work is the norm.

It turns well with all tools. It rarely exhibits interlocking grain, but when it does, grain tear-out is likely with all but the sharpest tools. It sands well, but will clog abrasives. It readily accepts penetrative finishes, but may be resistant to some surface finishes.

Brazilian rosewood
Dalbergia nigra

Other names Rio rosewood, Bahia rosewood, palisander, jacarandá, jacarandá da Bahia, jacarandá do Brasil

Grows South-eastern Brazil

Height up to 38m (125ft)

Trunk diameter 3–4ft (1–1.2m)

Specific gravity .85

Typical dry weight 53lb/ft³ (850kg/m³)

Possible health risks Dust may cause dermatitis, eye irritation and respiratory problems

Seasoning Brazilian rosewood is slow to dry, and liable to check and split. It is not available in large sizes, and is usually supplied air-dried in small pre-dimensioned blanks that I think are best rough-turned and set aside to stabilize or dry before finishing. It can be worked partially seasoned, but may check and will certainly move.

Characteristics This is an amazing wood to look at, and is mostly used for decorative or artistic work and in furniture restoration. It is a dense, heavy and hard wood with a waxy or oily feel to it. The heartwood is a reddish, dark chocolate-brown to rich purplish-brown colour with purplish-black and golden-brown streaks. The sapwood is fairly wide and creamy or greyish-white in colour. The grain is generally straight but sometimes wavy, with an even, fine texture, and capable of holding fine detail.

The wood cuts satisfactorily with all tools, though bevels may become gummed up with a wax-like resin which needs to be cleaned off every so often to keep them cutting – honing or resharpening will do this. Abrasives also clog readily, and the wood is prone to heat-checking. Wet sanding is not recommended. The wood resists some surface finishes but readily accepts penetrative finishes; these do not penetrate far, but they do polish the surface.

Honduras rosewood
Dalbergia stevensonii

Other names Nogaed, palisandro de Honduras

Grows Belize (formerly British Honduras)

Height 50–100ft (15–30m)

Trunk diameter 3ft (0.9m)

Specific gravity .96

Typical dry weight 60lb/ft³ (960kg/m³)

Possible health risks Dermatitis and asthma

Seasoning The wood air-dries very slowly with a risk of splitting, but it can be kiln-dried with little degrade. If undertaking restoration work, kiln-dried wood is sufficient; for decorative or artistic work, rough-turn the piece, coat with PVA and set aside to season.

Characteristics This is a beautiful wood with a sumptuous appearance. The heartwood ranges from light pinkish- or reddish-brown to deep reddish- or violet-brown, with lighter and darker irregular bands. The grain is usually straight but can be wavy. It has a medium to fine texture. The sapwood, which is distinct from the heartwood, is a pale cream when newly cut, but quickly darkens to yellow on exposure to light. Honduras rosewood is much prized by cabinetmakers and veneer companies, and wherever it is bought it is always expensive. Turners use it mostly for smallish decorative or artistic pieces. The colour contrast between sapwood and heartwood can be used to good visual effect.

The wood cuts best with bevel-rubbing tools, but a good finish can be obtained using a scraper in either conventional or shear-scraping mode. Some dust is produced when turning. Abrasives clog quickly, and the wood will heat-check if you are not careful. Wet sanding works well and produces a finer finish than dry sanding, as long as the sapwood is not present to cause colour contamination. It will take surface and penetrative finishes well, and can be taken to a very high polish.

African ebony
Diospyros crassiflora

Other names Cameroon, Gabon, Madagascar, Nigerian ebony

Grows Cameroon, Ghana, Nigeria, Congo

Height 50–60ft (15–18m)

Trunk diameter 2ft (0.6m)

Specific gravity 1.03

Typical dry weight 64lb/ft³ (1030kg/m³)

Possible health risks Dust may cause acute dermatitis, skin inflammation, conjunctivitis and sneezing

Seasoning Air-drying is quick and usually satisfactory, but there can be some surface checking. Part-seasoned wood can be turned to completion, as long as a fairly even wall thickness is maintained to avoid splitting. Work requiring accuracy must be rough-turned, coated with PVA and set aside to season.

Characteristics African ebonies are normally available only in short billets or small to medium-sized pre-dimensioned pieces of heartwood. *D. crassiflora* is the blackest, though even this can have some silver or grey in it. Other ebony species can have black and rich brown stripes in the heartwood. All these species are hard and dense, and the grain ranges from straight to interlocked, with a very fine, even texture. They have a severe blunting effect on cutting edges.

A fine finish can be produced off the tools and, unusually, scrapers can sometimes produce a better finish than bevel-rubbing tools. If the grain is interlocking, some tear-out may occur; very sharp tools will minimize this, but will not stop it completely. It is also somewhat brittle, so can splinter or fracture on or near sharp edges. It is a wood that can be power-carved to good effect. Note that a lot of noxious dust can be produced during turning. Sanding is OK if care is taken to avoid heat-checking, and the wood can be finished with surface or penetrative finishes. The light-coloured sapwood, if free from checks, can be effective as a visual contrast to the dark heartwood.

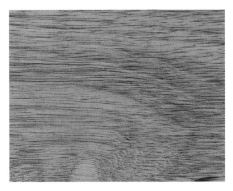

Persimmon
Diospyros virginiana

Other names American ebony, bara-bara, boa-wood, butterwood, possum wood, Virginia date palm, white ebony

Grows USA

Height 80–120ft (24–37m)

Trunk diameter 1–2ft (0.3–0.6m)

Specific gravity .83

Typical dry weight 52lb/ft³ (830kg/m³)

Possible health risks Heartwood may cause dermatitis

Seasoning This wood can be difficult to dry, suffering from considerable shrinkage, end and surface checks, and brown chemical staining. It moves significantly in service. It is a wood that I find turns well when wet – keep an even wall thickness and allow it to move as it likes – but I have had quite a high failure rate with rough-turning and setting it aside to season. I have tried varying the wall thickness – both thicker and thinner than I normally use – and the results are unpredictable.

Characteristics The heartwood forms only a small central core, and may be black or a rich red-brown. The sapwood, which makes up the majority of the timber, is creamy-white when freshly cut, darkening to yellow-brown or grey-brown on exposure, with brown or grey spots. The grain is quite close and straight, with a fine and even texture, and is capable of holding fine detail.

The wood turns well with any tools, as long as they are sharp, but bevel-rubbing tools produce a better finish than scrapers. Sanding is good, but heat-checking is likely if too much heat is generated. It will accept any finish of your choice.

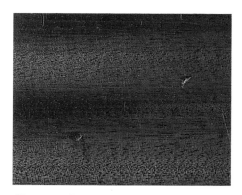

Sapele

Entandrophragma cylindricum

Other names Sapelewood, sapele mahogany, sapelli, scented mahogany, aboudikro, penkra

Grows West, central and east Africa to Uganda

Height up to 150ft (45m)

Trunk diameter 4–6ft (1.2–1.8m)

Specific gravity .62

Typical dry weight 39lb/ft³ (620kg/m³)

Possible health risks Skin irritation and sneezing

Seasoning It dries quickly, is prone to distortion and may surface-check a little. Kiln-dried timber is fine for most projects, but rough-turning and setting it aside to season works well also.

Characteristics The heartwood is reddish-yellow when first cut, darkening to a mid- to deep red or rich red-brown on exposure. The sapwood is cream to pale yellow but is rarely used. The grain is usually interlocked and wavy, which can create a fiddleback or mottle figure. It sometimes exhibits a very striking striped or roe figure on the quartercut surface. Sapele is a moderately hard and strong timber of medium density, with a fine and even texture. Used extensively in joinery and cabinetmaking, it offers many opportunities for turners to create components for these trades, as well as to explore its potential for artistic work. Since it is available in large sizes, there is plenty of scope to experiment.

This wood generally behaves itself during turning. but is prone to grain tear-out. Sharp bevel-rubbing tools will produce a better finish than scrapers. You may find it best to skip the scraper stage and go straight from gouges or skews to abrasives. Sapele can be sanded with either dry or wet sanding methods, and can be taken to a high polish with either surface or penetrative finishes.

Utile

Entandrophragma utile

Other names Assié, sipo, abebay, efuodwe, liboyo, kisi-kosi, afau-konkonti

Grows West, central and east Africa

Height 150–200ft (45–60m)

Trunk diameter 2ft 8in–6ft (0.8–1.8m)

Specific gravity .66

Typical dry weight 41lb/ft³ (660kg/m³)

Possible health risks Skin irritation

Seasoning Degrade is minimal, provided the wood is dried at a moderate rate; if dried too fast, it may twist. It can be turned from a partially seasoned state. Kiln-dried stock is sufficient when turning for joinery or cabinetmaking, but for greater accuracy it can be rough-turned and set aside to season.

Characteristics The sapwood is light brown, up to 2in (50mm) thick and clearly distinct from the heartwood. The latter is pinkish-brown, darkening to a deep red-brown or chocolate-brown on exposure. The grain is usually interlocked, with a medium texture. Quartersawn surfaces may have a ribbon figure or stripe, which can cause this wood to be mistaken for sapele (*E. cylindricum*). There can be other figuring such as rippling, but this is not so common.

Utile has a moderate blunting effect on edge tools, but as long as you maintain a good keen edge on your tools it will cut well. Small chips with quite a lot of dust will be produced with bevel-rubbing tools, but a good finish off the tool is possible. Scrapers will cause grain tear-out, and shear-scraping is not much better; instead, go straight to abrasive to remove minor blemishes left from the gouge or skew. It sands well and will readily accept finishes of all descriptions.

Australian eucalyptus burrs (burls)

Australian timbers are becoming increasingly popular with turners around the world. The burrs ('burls' in Australian and US usage) listed here all have similar characteristics. They are usually sold just as they have been cut off the tree, as a carbuncle-like piece which has one flat face; the other surfaces are all natural-edged, sometimes with bark still attached. Other pieces are supplied with the bark sandblasted off. Through-cut slabs or slices can also be bought.

Most of these burrs, I find, are best turned as they come, without further seasoning. My experience has mostly been with red mallee, York gum and coolibah, which are slow-growing and quite dry when bought anyway, though they do have some moisture in them – the pieces I had were at 15% moisture content when bought. If you are going to cut up the burr to make boxes and the like, then rough-turning and setting the piece aside to season works well. You may find that you need to coat the piece with PVA to even out the stabilizing process. Burrs which are very old and dry may produce a lot of dust during turning.

Since the working qualities of these timbers are mostly very similar, only red mallee (*Eucalyptus oleosa*, *E. socialis*) has been described in detail; it is a representative example of the harder, denser eucalyptus burrs.

Possible health risks Not known; but do take precautions to minimize exposure to dust

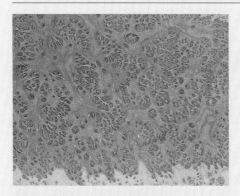

Brown mallee
Eucalyptus spp.

Grows Not known
Typical burr size 13–15lb (6–7kg)
Characteristics Brown mallee burr is dense, hard, heavy and oily. The heartwood is tan-coloured and the sapwood is a creamy grey-white. The burr figuring commonly consists of various-sized clusters of tightly packed pippy knots or 'eyes', and the grain is tight and interlocked. There is much colour variation from piece to piece.

Being oily, it is reasonably easy to cut with bevel-rubbing tools, producing some nice shavings as well as chips. It scrapes well with minimal grain tear-out, provided sensitive cuts are made with sharp tools. Tear-out may occur, but is not as pronounced as in some other species. It clogs abrasives quite quickly, so regular cleaning of them is necessary. Being dense and oily, it accepts hand-chased threads reasonably well.

Oil finish

Ridge-fruited mallee
Eucalyptus angulosa and *E. incrassata*

Grows Western Australia and South Australia
Typical burr size 13–15lb (6–7kg)
Characteristics Ridge-fruited mallee burr is dense, hard and heavy, with irregular or interlocking grain. The heartwood is a rich red with hints of orange, tan and violet-brown. The sapwood is pinkish-cream. The burr figuring is best described as dramatic, and often has big whorls and streaks in various hues of the heartwood colour.

It works and responds to turning in the same way as red mallee (*E. oleosa*, *E. socialis*).

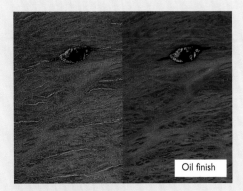

Oil finish

Coolibah
Eucalyptus coolabah, syn. *E. microtheca*
Other names Also spelt **coolabah**

Grows From Northern Territory to Western Australia and Queensland
Typical burr size 18–26lb (8–12kg)
Characteristics Coolibah is the hardest of the burrs discussed on these pages, and is reputed to be one of the hardest woods available. It can replace lignum vitae (*Guaiacum officinale*) in some situations. It works in much the same way as red mallee (*E. oleosa, E. socialis*), but owing to its hardness it is a bit more difficult to work and slower to cut, producing chips and frequently some dust as well. Because of the irregular, interlocking grain it is very likely to suffer from tear-out. The heartwood is a rich milk-chocolate colour which contrasts well with the creamy-tan sapwood. The figuring tends to consist of wavy, swirling whorls, interspersed with pips or 'eyes' which look like elongated bubbles; it can have darker irregular flecks running through it.

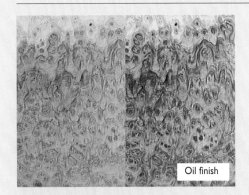

Oil finish

York gum
Eucalyptus loxophleba

Grows Goldfields region of Western Australia
Typical burr size 13–15lb (6–7kg)
Characteristics York gum burr is extremely hard and dense, which is due in part to the conditions in which it grows. It works in the same manner as red mallee (*E. oleosa, E. socialis*). The heartwood is a greyish- or reddish-tan colour and the sapwood creamy-tan, but the colour varies somewhat from one piece to another. The burr figuring is a loose pippy formation with some wavy or twisted swirling patterns. It is a fantastic wood to look at, but moderately difficult to work. York gum and many other species are sometimes marketed under the general name of **Goldfield burrs**.

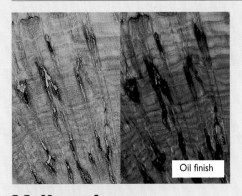

Oil finish

Yellow box
Eucalyptus melliodora

Grows Victoria and New South Wales
Typical burr size 18–20lb (8–9kg)
Characteristics Yellow box burr has a very attractive figure. It is dense and cuts well. It has a slightly oily nature, and is close-grained. It typically has gum pockets irregularly placed amongst whorls, or swirling or wavy grain. The sapwood is grey-brown, a little darker than the heartwood, which is a yellow-tan colour with a reddish-orange tinge. It has a higher moisture content than other burrs listed here, so care is needed when drying: part-turn the piece and seal with PVA to even out the drying process, then set it aside to season further. You can turn it from partially seasoned stock, but expect more movement than one gets with the other eucalyptus species. It turns well, and shavings are produced when cutting this wood. It sands and finishes well also.

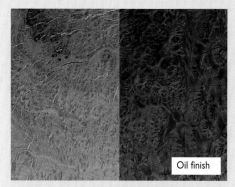

Oil finish

Western grey box
Eucalyptus microcarpa

Grows South Australia
Typical burr size 13–15lb (6–7kg)
Characteristics Western grey box is very similar to brown mallee in working quality. It has more pips or knots than swirling grain. The sapwood is greyish-white and the heartwood a mid-orange-tan; a distinct narrow grey line separates the two. This is a visually stunning burr that will respond well to a bit of love and care in working it.

Red mallee
Eucalyptus oleosa and *E. socialis*
Other names Oil mallee, giant mallee

Grows Western Australia
Typical burr size 13–15lb (6–7kg)
Characteristics Red mallee burrs are dense, hard, heavy, close-grained and slightly oily. The wood has a greyish-cream sapwood which is distinct from the reddish-tan or brown heartwood. That said, the burr figuring – which is often a beautiful swirling whorl pattern – has various orange or reddish-tan hues in it. Depending on how it is cut, the figuring can show as dramatic striations.

There is a lot of interlocking grain, which means that tools produce chips rather than shavings. Grain tear-out is a distinct possibility around the figured areas. Because of its hardness, this timber belongs to that rare group of woods where you may find it easier to scrape than to use a gouge or other bevel-rubbing tool. If a scraper is used sensitively, it is possible to get a smooth surface finish with minimal grain tear-out. As with many other Australian burrs, cutting edges do not last long, so frequent sharpening will be necessary. For artistic or decorative work, or for natural-edged pieces, this burr can be used in large slabs. When it dries fully the surface of the timber tends to take on a 'hammered' texture, more so than brown mallee.

It is a hard wood to sand, so get as good a finish off the tool as you can before sanding. Do not be tempted to skip grades, but work through them all to achieve a very fine finish. It can be finished with oils, waxes or surface finishes as you require; my preference is for oils, which I find bring out the figuring beautifully. I find that the wood darkens a little with age, but the fantastic figuring will still be visible. This is not an easy wood to turn, but the effort will be well rewarded.

Bowl by Bert Marsh

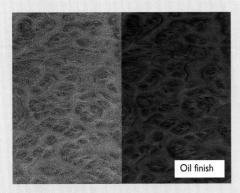

Oil finish

Red box
Eucalyptus polyanthemos

Grows Central and southern tablelands, New South Wales, Victoria
Typical burr size 26–33lb (12–15kg)
Characteristics I love working with burrs and figured wood of all varieties, and this is one of the nicest you are likely to encounter. Red box burr is harder than yellow box (*E. melliodora*) burr. It is a tight, pippy, 'eyed' burr, but this may be combined with other formations such as wavy or swirling patterns. It has a warm brownish-red heartwood and a softer, lighter-coloured sapwood which contrasts well with the richer heartwood.

Its turning qualities are a hybrid between those of red mallee (*E. oleosa, E. socialis*) and yellow box.

Platter by Simon Hope

Salmon gum
Eucalyptus salmonophloia

Grows Western Australia
Typical burr size 26–31lb (12–14kg)
Characteristics Salmon gum burr is what is termed a 'resin-gum burl', which means that there are gum pockets in the wood. These show as voids or fissures which may have a lining of resin, or be completely filled with resin. The resin appears black to the eye, but when a light is shone on it it can be a very deep red or amber. It is hard, and blunts tool edges quickly. The resin pockets and various sizes of fissures will fill up with sanding dust and finishing material, so they need to be carefully cleaned out to create a consistent, clean-looking finish. The burr itself is a deep, rich red-brown colour that has a twisted, swirling grain formation. It sometimes has darker flecks running through it.

Apart from the gum pockets, it behaves for the most part in a similar way to red mallee (*E. oleosa, E. socialis*).

Oil finish

Gimlet
Eucalyptus salubris
Other names Gimlet gum

Grows Western Australia
Typical burr size 26–31lb (12–14kg)
Characteristics Gimlet burr has light creamy-golden sapwood and rich reddish-brown heartwood irregularly interspersed with darker patches. Swirls and twisting patterns are common, flecked with little pockets of resin gum. It works in much the same way as red mallee (*E. oleosa, E. socialis*), but being less oily it does not cut quite as cleanly. The wood is dense, hard and heavy, like all the eucalyptus burrs mentioned here. The grain is fine and even in texture but extremely erratic – some parts interlocked, others twisted – which is typical of many burrs.

Rather than using proprietary finishes out of the can, you could tint a plain oil or surface finish by adding powdered dyes or artists' oil colours to it. With any of the burrs mentioned here, these tinted finishes can be used to highlight and enhance the figuring. You could try staining or dyeing the wood directly, but these timbers are so dense that, in my experience, the finish is bound to be very patchy as a result of uneven penetration.

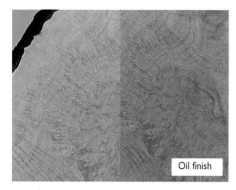

Oil finish

Briar burr (burl)

Erica arborea

Other names Not known

Grows South-west Europe

Height and diameter Not known; sold as root burrs for turning, typically 8 × 8 × 6in (200 × 200 × 150mm)

Specific gravity 0.75

Typical dry weight 4kg for a piece 200 × 200 × 150mm

Possible health risks Not known

Seasoning The roots are boiled after harvesting to prevent splitting and to retain colour. They can be turned to completion straight away, but the wall thickness must be thin and even to minimize the risk of cracking. Alternatively, the burr can be rough-turned and set aside to season; coating with PVA reduces cracking and checking. Leave the wet root structure too long, though, and it can rot in the centre.

Characteristics The roots are mid-brown with a reddish-orange tinge, with some lighter and darker patches. They can have a fantastic swirling, twisting grain figure, or a more mottled, tightly swirled pattern. Each piece is unique, and I have yet to find one that I did not like. They respond well to dyes, which can increase the visibility and contrast of the figuring phenomenally.

These roots are wonderful to turn and carve, especially when wet or partially seasoned. The wood cuts very easily with all tools, but the best cuts are made with gouges and skews. It sands and polishes well. Old wood can be dusty and a bit brittle, in contrast to freshly seasoned sections. The biggest drawback is the irregular shape and size: you need to be careful in your selection to make sure that you can obtain the required profile. I find them very effective for hollow-form projects: the irregular shapes may give rise to natural-edged voids which have great visual appeal. Watch out for any embedded stones: if you do not remove them straight away they can whizz off the rotating workpiece at high speed.

Tamboti

Excoecaria africana, syn. *Spirostachys africana*

Other names Tambooti, African sandalwood

Grows Southern and eastern Africa

Height 50ft (15m)

Trunk diameter 2ft (0.6m)

Specific gravity .80

Typical dry weight 50lb/ft³ (800kg/m³)

Possible health risks Bark exudes a sticky sap which is highly irritant to skin and eyes, but this is removed when timber is dimensioned. Wood can cause severe skin irritation. It taints food when used as a cooking fuel

Seasoning It seasons well if dried slowly. I have only been able to obtain air-dried pieces, some of which were quite wet and required further seasoning. It can be turned wet or partially seasoned to completion, and moves a little but not much. It also responds well to rough-turning and setting aside to season, but because of its oil content this takes a fair while — longer than ash or oak (*Fraxinus*, *Quercus* spp.), for instance. Coat the rough-turned piece with PVA to even out the drying and minimize splitting — I had a few failures before I tried this.

Characteristics This beautiful wood is heavy, dense and richly coloured. The heartwood has bands of light and dark reddish, honeyed browns. The narrow sapwood is a light, creamy butter colour — a truly lovely mix. The grain is generally straight but can be interlocked and wavy. It is capable of holding quite fine detail. I have worked with wet, partially seasoned and dry wood without suffering the adverse reactions mentioned opposite, but I do find that the dust aggravates my rhinitis. I use this wood only for decorative items, and would advise you to do the same.

It cuts well with all tools, but there is a fair amount of oily dust produced during the cut and when sanding, so good extraction is a must. A good finish straight off the tool is possible, provided very sharp tools are used with a slow, deliberate cut. Frequent sharpening will be necessary. It sands satisfactorily, but clogs the abrasive quickly and is prone to heat-checking. It finishes well.

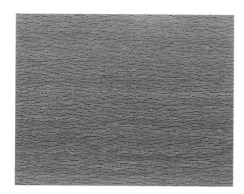

American beech

Fagus grandifolia

Other names Beech

Grows Eastern Canada and USA

Height 150ft (45m)

Trunk diameter 4ft (1.2m)

Specific gravity .74

Typical dry weight 46lb/ft³ (740kg/m³)

Possible health risks Dermatitis, eye irritation, decrease in lung function, rare incidence of nasal cancer

Seasoning Care is needed in drying, because the wood dries rapidly and tends to split, warp and surface-check. There can be a substantial amount of shrinkage, and the wood may discolour. It can be wet-turned, or rough-turned and set aside to season further. Joinery and cabinetmaking parts can usually be turned satisfactorily from kilned stock.

Characteristics The narrow sapwood is off-white with a pink tinge, while the heartwood is light to dark reddish-brown. American beech tends to be slightly darker and less consistent than European beech (*F. sylvatica*). It occasionally forms burrs and ripple figure, but otherwise it is a somewhat bland timber. It is available in large sizes and has a close, uniform texture. The grain is usually straight, but can be interlocked. These qualities make it an excellent choice for turned components in joinery and cabinetmaking, for artistic work, and – because there is no smell or taste with this wood – domestic utilitarian ware.

Apart from some end-grain tear-out, usually when using scrapers in conventional cutting mode, this wood is a pleasure to work with. It cuts very cleanly with gouges and skews, and may require only a very light sanding to remove blemishes. It sands and polishes well and can be brought to a high polish if needed.

American ash

Fraxinus americana, F. pennsylvanica and *F. nigra*

Other names White ash, northern ash, southern ash (*F. americana*); green ash, red ash (*F. pennsylvanica*); black ash, brown ash (*F. nigra*)

Grows Canada and eastern USA

Height 80–120ft (25–36m)

Trunk diameter 2–5ft (0.6–1.5m)

Specific gravity .66 (*F. nigra* .56)

Typical dry weight 41lb/ft³ (660kg/m³) (*F. nigra* 35lb/ft³ (560kg/m³))

Possible health risks Rhinitis, asthma, decrease in lung function

Seasoning It dries fairly easily with minimal degrade, and there is little movement in use. Grey-brown stains and surface checks can occur. Wet-turning to completion, working from partially seasoned stock, or rough-turning and setting it aside to season are all feasible routes to explore.

Characteristics American white ash, in particular, is a wonderful wood to work with. It does not shout its presence, is very attractive. It looks similar to European ash (*F. excelsior*), but is a little less dense. The sapwood is off-white, and the heartwood can vary from pale cream or tan to dark brown with a pinkish tinge. The other two species vary in colour from a light greyish-tan to grey-brown, but all have similar working qualities. The grain is generally straight, with a coarse but uniform texture. It is generally available as through-cut boards and pre-dimensioned blanks, and can be found in reasonably large sizes. It is suitable for joinery and cabinetmaking components, artistic and functional ware.

This wood cuts best with bevel-rubbing tools, producing a nice finish off the tool. Scrapers work fine – shear-scraping produces a better finish than conventional scraping – but can rough up the end grain. It sands well, and you can stain and polish it to a very good finish.

Maracaibo boxwood

Gossypiospermum praecox

Other names Zapatero, palo blanco, agracejo; also Colombian, Venezuelan, West Indian boxwood

Grows Venezuela, Colombia, Dominican Republic

Height up to 30ft (10m)

Trunk diameter 8–16in (0.2–0.4m)

Specific gravity .85

Typical dry weight 53lb/ft³ (850kg/m³)

Possible health risks Not known

Seasoning This wood dries slowly and is quite difficult to air-dry. Splitting and surface checking are common, and blue staining is also possible if conditions are humid. Halve stock longitudinally or dimension it before drying to prevent splitting. It can be turned to completion from wet, partially seasoned or kilned stock, but, if accuracy is required for items such as lidded boxes, then rough-turning and setting it aside to season is a must.

Characteristics The heartwood and sapwood look similar to each other, and can be anything from off-white to butter-yellow or lemon-yellow. The grain is mostly straight, the texture fine, uniform and compact. It can be used as a replacement for boxwood (*Buxus sempervirens*) in most circumstances but lacks the density of true boxwood. It holds very fine detail, but is certainly inferior to true boxwood in its ability to hold a screw thread. Uses include inlay, stringing, chess pieces, bobbins, piano keys, woodwind instruments, carving and fine decorative turnings. This wood cuts like a dream. Both bevel-rubbing tools and scrapers can give a good finish off the tool which requires very little sanding. It takes finishes readily and can be brought to a high polish if required.

Ovangkol

Guibourtia ehie

Other names Ovengkol, amazaque, amazakoué, anokye, ehie, shedua, hyeduanini

Grows Gabon, Ghana, Ivory Coast, Nigeria

Height 100–150ft (30–45m)

Trunk diameter 2–3ft (0.6–0.9m)

Specific gravity .80

Typical dry weight 50lb/ft³ (800kg/m³)

Possible health risks Not known

Seasoning It seasons quickly and well, with little degrade, but is difficult to kiln-dry. It can be wet-turned, but is more commonly turned partially seasoned or kilned. It moves a little, but not much. It can be rough-turned and set aside to season; coating with PVA minimizes the risk of end-grain splits.

Characteristics An attractive wood whose heartwood ranges from a golden honey-brown to dark reddish-brown, with greyish or deep violet-black stripes. The grain is straight or interlocked, with a moderately coarse texture. It sometimes has an attractive figure, ripple, roey or mottled, especially on quartersawn surfaces. The distinct creamy-white sapwood is about 4in (100mm) thick. Ovangkol is available in reasonable sizes. The shavings will stain metal and hands, so be sure to clean up thoroughly after turning.

The wood turns satisfactorily but, despite its density, the end grain and figured areas are likely to suffer tear-out; sharp bevel-rubbing tools will minimize this but not prevent it completely. Scrapers in shear-scraping or conventional mode do not produce as good a finish, but may help in removing blemishes. There is a risk of splintering at the edges of the work. Seasoned wood produces a fair amount of dust. I use bevel-rubbing tools to get as good a finish as I can, and then go straight to abrasives. The wood sands well enough either wet or dry, but avoid the wet method if sapwood is present. It takes surface or penetrative finishes well. Though it can be tricky to work, the results are worth the effort.

Butternut

Juglans cinerea

Other names White walnut, oilnut, nogal, nogal blanco, nuez meca

Grows Canada and USA

Height 40–70ft (12–21m)

Trunk diameter 1–2ft (0.3–0.6m)

Specific gravity .45

Typical dry weight 28lb/ft³ (450kg/m³)

Possible health risks Skin and eye irritation

Seasoning Butternut dries slowly with minimal shrinkage or degrade, and is fairly stable in use. It needs to be air-dried thoroughly before kilning. Alternatively, it can be wet-turned to completion or rough-turned and set aside to season further.

Characteristics This is a light, soft timber. The heartwood is light reddish-brown, often featuring darker reddish-brown streaks. The sapwood is usually about 1in (25mm) wide and can range from off-white to a light, creamy grey-brown. Butternut has straight grain, with a medium to coarse, but soft texture and the lustre of satin. Ripple or mottled figure is sometimes present, but not common. Fungal stain colouring can be present, adding another dimension to what is otherwise a relatively bland-looking wood. It is not available in very big sizes, but is great for small decorative or utilitarian work. It is also nice to carve with hand or power tools.

This soft timber is easy to work with sharp bevel-rubbing tools, but does not respond well to the use of a scraper, in either conventional or shear-scraping mode. It is best to skip scrapers and go straight from gouges and skews to abrasives. Butternut sands well and finishes well with surface or penetrative finishes, but can be a little 'hungry', so it may require a few coats to achieve an even coverage.

Virginian pencil cedar

Juniperus virginiana

Other names Pencil cedar, red cedar, eastern red cedar, juniper, savin

Grows Canada and USA

Height 40–60ft (12–18m)

Trunk diameter 1–2ft (0.3–0.6m)

Specific gravity .53

Typical dry weight 33lb/ft³ (530kg/m³)

Possible health risks Not known

Seasoning Slow seasoning is needed to prevent end splitting and fine surface checking. It can be turned to completion wet, partially seasoned or kiln-dried, if you can obtain suitable pieces. Alternatively, it can be rough-turned and set aside for further seasoning. If, however, the work in hand does not demand great accuracy, work straight from the piece you have.

Characteristics This colourful and beautiful softwood is really nice to work with. The heartwood is light pink, mid-red or violet-red, but darkens to a dull orange-red or mid-brown with age. There may be small knots. The narrow sapwood is light cream. Virginian pencil cedar has fine, even, straight grain and a fine texture. Though not a true cedar, it has a cedar-like scent, which can be quite 'heady' in confined spaces. It is not available in large sizes and is usually bought as through-cut boards or pre-dimensioned blanks. It can be used for joinery, cabinetmaking, decorative and utilitarian turning, but because of the scent from its natural oils it is not recommended for items which may come into contact with food. This is a wood that can be carved.

This wood cuts well with sharp bevel-rubbing tools, giving a very good finish. Scrapers are likely to cause torn grain, so use gouges and skews, then go straight to abrasive. It sands well with wet or dry methods. It readily takes both surface and penetrative finishes, but oil finishes impart a wonderful, warm yellow colour, further enhancing what is already a beautifully coloured wood.

Laburnum

Laburnum anagyroides

Other names Golden chain

Grows Central and southern Europe

Height 20–30ft (6–9m)

Trunk diameter 1ft (0.3m)

Specific gravity .82

Typical dry weight 52lb/ft³ (820kg/m³)

Possible health risks Seeds are highly toxic to humans and animals

Seasoning It dries easily, but slow drying is recommended to prevent end-checking and splitting. Partially seasoned or wet wood can be turned to completion, or it can be rough-turned, coated with PVA and set aside to season. Trees and boughs are hard to season whole, so part-turning is recommended.

Characteristics The heartwood is bright yellow-brown with a green tinge when freshly cut, but darkens to a rich golden-brown, then deep purplish- or red-brown, and eventually a deep, rich dark brown. The sapwood is narrow and creamy-white. Laburnum usually has straight grain, a fairly fine texture and a lustrous surface. It is hard and dense. There is a pleasing growth-ring figure when it is flatsawn, and a fleck pattern when quartersawn. It holds quite fine detail and can be carved with hand or power tools. It is prized for decorative and utilitarian work, furniture parts, and parts of musical instruments; also for veneers and inlay, including cross-grain 'oysters'. Not available in very big sizes, it is usually bought as a whole trunk or bough, or as pre-dimensioned blanks.

The finest finish off the tool is achieved with skews and gouges. Scrapers can cause tear-out, especially on end grain; if you must use them, shear-scraping is best. The wood sands well wet or dry, but avoid the wet method if sapwood is present. There may be some heat-checking if too much heat is generated. A high finish can be obtained with either oils or surface finishes. Oil darkens the wood considerably, but imparts a warm glow when burnished.

Huon pine

Lagarostrobos franklinii, syn. *Dacrydium franklinii*

Other names White pine, Macquarie pine

Grows South-western Tasmania

Height 65–125ft (20–38m)

Trunk diameter 3ft 3in–6ft (1–1.8m)

Specific gravity .52

Typical dry weight 32lb/ft³ (520kg/m³)

Possible health risks Not known

Seasoning A very stable timber, favoured for boatbuilding due to its stability and low shrinkage. It dries readily but tends to suffer slight surface checking. It can be turned wet or partially seasoned, or can be rough-turned and set aside for further seasoning.

Characteristics This handsome softwood has pale, narrow sapwood, not very distinct from the heartwood, which is light cream to buttery brown. Huon pine has straight grain, with fine, closely spaced growth rings, giving it a fine and even texture. It is quite a light, soft wood with fair strength. It is oily when freshly worked, and this essential oil, methyl eugenol, helps it to resist decay and attack by lyctus borers. The oil has a pleasant smell and helps the wood to cut cleanly. Huon pine can be used for decorative and utilitarian pieces, and carves well. However, since logging is controlled for environmental reasons, it is difficult to get hold of and usually commands a very high price.

This is an easy wood to work with gouges and skews. Scrapers are likely to cause end-grain tear-out. It sands satisfactorily but can clog abrasives and is vulnerable to heat-checking. It can be sanded wet or dry. It accepts most finishes well, but due to its oil content it may resist some surface finishes.

American red gum

Liquidambar styraciflua

Other names Gum, sweetgum, sapgum, redgum, star-leafed gum, alligator tree, alligator wood, liquidambar, hazel pine, bilsted, satin walnut

Grows USA

Height 80–120ft (24–36m)

Trunk diameter 2–3ft (0.6–0.9m)

Specific gravity .56

Typical dry weight 35lb/ft³ (560kg/m³)

Possible health risks Dermatitis

Seasoning Thick pieces may tend to warp during the early stages of drying, but it can generally be air- or kiln-dried without problems – though splitting may occur if it is dried too fast. Architectural, joinery or cabinetmaking turnery can be done with kiln-dried wood, but if you need accuracy then rough-turning and setting it aside to season is a must. Alternatively, if you can obtain boughs, sections of trunk, or partially seasoned pieces, these can be turned wet or partially seasoned to completion.

Characteristics The heartwood is mid-brown with red tints, and may have dark streaks. The sapwood is wide, and creamy-yellow with a hint of red. The grain is often irregular and interlocked, and may exhibit a ribbon stripe. The texture is uniform, and this attractive wood has a lustre like satin. Many pieces have a fine figure. You may find the heartwood sold as **redgum** or **figured redgum**; the sapwood may be sold separately as **sapgum**.

This timber is especially easy to work and only slightly affects the cutting edges of your tools, but it cuts best with bevel-rubbing tools. It is a nice wood to carve as well as turn. It sands well with the dry sanding method; wet sanding should only be undertaken if no sapwood is present. It will accept any finish of your choice. Try it – you won't be disappointed.

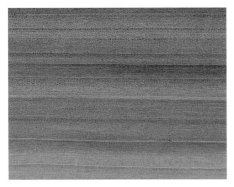

American tulipwood

Liriodendron tulipifera

Other names Yellow poplar, white poplar, tulip poplar, tulip tree, whitewood, canary whitewood, canoe wood, saddletree. Unrelated to Brazilian tulipwood (*Dalbergia frutescens*)

Grows Throughout eastern USA

Height 80–120ft (24–37m)

Trunk diameter 2–3ft (0.6–0.9m)

Specific gravity .51

Typical dry weight 31lb/ft³ (510kg/m³)

Possible health risks Dermatitis

Seasoning This timber air-dries and kiln-dries very well, normally without degrade. If dried too slowly, sapwood stains and mould can develop. Depending on what sections you buy, it can be wet-turned successfully, or set aside to season after rough-turning. But for the majority of projects that are likely to be undertaken with this wood you can get away with working kiln-dried or partially seasoned wood to completion.

Characteristics The sapwood is off-white, often with streaks, while the heartwood varies from pale yellow-brown to olive-green-brown, and may be streaked with blue-green, red-purple or brown-black. The light green colour of fresh-cut heartwood tends to darken to a mid green-brown on exposure to light. Grain is straight and texture is medium to fine. This wood is widely used in joinery, and is usually painted or stained in these applications. It can be used for decorative work, and it carves well, but it is a bland wood without much inherent visual appeal. Since it takes paint, stain or spray lacquer well, you could consider using colour in your work, perhaps together with carving.

It works well with bevel-rubbing tools. Scrapers will more likely than not tear out the grain. It sands well, though many textbooks suggest otherwise; I have been able to achieve a very fine finish by sanding through the grades down to 400 grit or finer. It takes finishes well, but may require a few coats to ensure even coverage.

African walnut

Lovoa trichilioides

Other names Benin walnut, Nigerian golden walnut, Ghana walnut, alona wood, bibolo, congowood, eyan, lovoa, nivero noy

Grows Tropical west Africa

Height 150ft (45m)

Trunk diameter 4ft (1.2m)

Specific gravity .56

Typical dry weight 35lb/ft³ (560kg/m³)

Possible health risks Irritation to mucous membranes and alimentary tract; nasal cancer

Seasoning It dries readily with little degrade whether kiln- or air-dried, though there may be some distortion and existing shakes are likely to extend. Heart shakes are common. Movement is usually slight, but sometimes it may shrink quite a bit. The wood is best rough-turned and then seasoned further. The sections usually available are boards or pre-dimensioned blanks, either part-seasoned or kiln-dried. Part-seasoned blanks can be turned to completion, but will distort a little.

Characteristics This lovely wood is not a true walnut. The sapwood, separated from the heartwood by a narrow transition zone, is a creamy-tan colour. The heartwood is a rich honey-brown with dark purplish-black gum lines. The grain is usually interlocked but can be straight, and has a fine texture with distinct growth rings. Quartersawn surfaces can exhibit a ribbon figure with alternating areas of darker and lighter wood. It is used in joinery, cabinetmaking and decorative turning.

The wood cuts well with most tools, but produces much dust. Scrapers are likely to tear the grain, but if they are very sharp you may get away with only a little sanding. Shear-scraping will minimize tear-out. It can be carved, preferably with power tools. It sands well either wet or dry, but if using the wet method make sure there is no sapwood present to cause colour contamination. It takes finishes readily and can be polished to a high gloss if needed; for a super-smooth finish the grain will need filling.

Santos rosewood

Machaerium scleroxylon

Other names Not known

Grows Bolivia

Height Medium-sized tree

Trunk diameter 1ft 8in (0.5m)

Specific gravity .85

Typical dry weight 53lb/ft³ (850kg/m³)

Possible health risks Dust can cause skin and nasal irritation

Seasoning It dries slowly and tends to suffer surface checks. It can be turned partially seasoned to completion, but will move, sometimes quite a lot. For lidded boxes or other precise work, rough-turning and setting aside to season is a must; coating rough-turned pieces with PVA will minimize checking.

Characteristics The heartwood ranges from light pink-brown to violet-brown, streaked with lighter and darker tones of brown and reddish-brown. The sapwood is narrow, and pale cream in colour. The grain texture is fine and uniform, occasionally interlocking.

This wood blunts cutting edges quickly and is difficult to saw, but is far easier to work on the lathe. Sharp tools and a delicate cut are necessary to minimize grain damage. Scrapers do not, on the whole, create as good a finish as bevel-rubbing tools, but with a freshly honed edge in shear-scraping mode you can achieve a surface that needs only the lightest touch with abrasives to clean it up. When turning or sanding, take care not to generate too much heat, or heat-checking may occur. A fair amount of dust may be created, so take sensible precautions to limit exposure to it. It finishes well with surface or penetrative finishes.

Magnolia
Magnolia grandiflora

Other names Evergreen magnolia, southern magnolia, mountain magnolia, sweet magnolia, cucumber wood, black lin, bat tree, big laurel, bullbay

Grows USA; cultivated in UK

Height 60–80ft (18–24m)

Trunk diameter 2–3ft (0.6–0.9m)

Specific gravity .56

Typical dry weight 35lb/ft³ (560kg/m³)

Possible health risks Not known

Seasoning Magnolia is generally best kiln-dried, when it will suffer from little degrade. Air-drying makes it shrink excessively, warp and check, and this tendency to distort can be exploited to good effect by wet-turning to a thin, even wall thickness. Turning partially seasoned wood will also result in movement. It can also be rough-turned and set aside for further drying; but allow an extra ¼in (6mm) or so of wall thickness per 12in (300mm) diameter to take account of the increased movement.

Characteristics The sapwood is a pale yellow-white. The heartwood is a light creamy-green tinged with tan, although it can be a little darker, bordering on mid-brown, often with dark reddish-violet streaks caused by mineral deposits. The grain is straight, with a regular fine, close texture. Magnolia can be used for utilitarian and decorative turning. There are also turning applications within the joinery and cabinetmaking trades. It can be carved with hand or power tools.

This wood turns well with skews and gouges, but does not respond well to conventional scraping, which will result in grain tear-out; shear-scraping is a little better, but not much. It is best to use the skew or gouge, depending on the type of work being undertaken, and then go straight to abrasives to remove any blemishes. It sands well, but be careful to keep the abrasive moving to avoid creating hollows. It takes surface or penetrative finishes well.

Apple
Malus sylvestris, syn. *M. pumila,*
Pyrus malus

Other names Not known. Crab apple (various *Malus* spp.) provides similar wood

Grows Temperate zones worldwide, and cooler areas of tropical regions

Height 25–50ft (8–15m)

Trunk diameter 1–2ft (0.3–0.6m)

Specific gravity .70

Typical dry weight 43lb/ft³ (700kg/m³)

Possible health risks Not known

Seasoning It dries slowly, and air-drying will more likely than not result in distortion. Apple can be kiln-dried with little degrade. It can be turned wet or partially seasoned to completion; the bark is thin and will stay in place if you want to include it on natural-edge work. Or you could rough-turn it and set it aside to season.

Characteristics The heartwood is between pink, beige and orange in colour. The grain is usually straight, occasionally irregular or interlocking, with a fine, even texture. It is capable of holding fine detail, and can be carved with hand or power tools. As with many fruitwoods, the roots are great to turn, if they are big enough, but they must be dried carefully so as not to split. The colour of the root timber is very varied, from a reddish-tan or orange to a dark reddish-brown.

Like other fruitwoods, this is a pleasure to turn. It responds well to all tools as long as the grain is straight and even. If there is irregular grain present, then scrapers may tear out the grain. It sands and finishes well.

Mango
Mangifera indica

Other names Manga, mangue, manako, mangot

Grows India, China, south-east Asia, West Indies, USA (Florida, Hawaii), Mexico, Peru, Brazil, South Africa

Height 65–100ft (20–30m)

Trunk diameter 3ft (1m)

Specific gravity .51

Typical dry weight 32lb/ft³ (510kg/m³)

Possible health risks Not known

Seasoning Mango is best kiln-dried swiftly after felling, as it is prone to fungal staining if air-dried. On the other hand, the colours in the fungal-stained wood can be very pleasant. It is a great wood for wet-turning to completion; or, if accuracy is required, it can be rough-turned and set aside to season further. Kiln-dried stock is fine for joinery or furniture turnings.

Characteristics Like many fruitwoods, this is a wonderful wood to work with and to look at. Mango is usually a soft buttery-brown to light tan, with dark wavy flecks where the pores are exposed, giving a marbled look. There may also be long bands of light creamy-red running through the wood. The texture is fine to medium, and the grain is sometimes wavy. It is capable of holding very fine detail, and is a nice wood to carve. Sadly, because the trees are grown for their fruit and not for the wood, it is not commonly available. It is used in the areas where it grows, but only occasionally does it get distributed further afield. I have had the privilege to turn a few pieces, and it was a real joy; I would love to get my hands on some more. It can be used for decorative and utilitarian turning.

The wood cuts well with all tools, although a better finish off the tool is achieved with bevel-rubbing tools. The only times that grain tear-out seems to occur is when interlocking grain is present, which is not common. The wood sands well, accepts finishes readily and can be finished to a high polish.

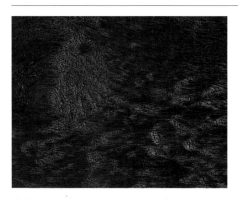

Honduras walnut
Metopium brownei

Other names Chechem, cachin, chechen, coral sumac, poison wood, black poison wood

Grows Cuba, Jamaica, northern Guatemala, Belize, Mexico, Dominican Republic

Height up to 50ft (15m)

Trunk diameter Not known

Specific gravity .64

Typical dry weight 40lb/ft³ (640kg/m³)

Possible health risks Black, caustic sap from freshly felled wood causes a reaction akin to that of poison ivy

Seasoning This wood is usually air-dried locally; once cut, dried and debarked, it is considered to be reasonably safe to work with. The blanks I have had were kiln-dried. I rough-turned them, coated them with PVA and set them aside to season. There was not much movement, and no splitting or end checking.

Characteristics This is a hard, dense, very attractive wood. I must admit that the health warnings on this wood worried me, but the working of it was fine and I suffered no reactions. I have only used the wood for decorative pieces. The heartwood is deep reddish- or purplish-brown. The sapwood is generally a creamy honey-brown with occasional soft red and green hues, and is clearly distinct from the heartwood. There is often a beautiful grain pattern, and the texture is fine and uniform.

The wood works fine with very sharp tools, but produces dust which some people may react to. Scrapers and dull tools can cause end-grain tear-out, but freshly honed scrapers work fine on most occasions; shear-scraping minimizes the risk. Sanding is fine; I recommend using only dry sanding and a surface finish, such as melamine lacquer. The oils I have tried darkened the wood considerably: in time it went almost black.

Bowl by
Bert Marsh

Zebrano
Microberlinia brazzavillensis and
M. bisulcata

Other names Zebrawood, African
zebrawood, zingana

Grows West Africa, mainly Cameroon and
Gabon

Height 150ft (45m)

Trunk diameter 4–5ft (1.2–1.5m)

Specific gravity .74

Typical dry weight 46lb/ft³ (740kg/m³)

Possible health risks Irritation to eyes
and skin

Seasoning This is difficult to dry. Kiln-drying and air-drying can be
used, but splitting, checking and distortion are possible if it is dried
too quickly. Trunk and branch wood can be wet-turned to
completion, in which case some movement will occur; but you
will more likely than not be working from part-seasoned blanks
with variable moisture content. If accuracy is required, rough-turn
the piece and set it aside to season further, coating with PVA to
retard moisture loss if you wish. The part-seasoned pieces have a
strange musty smell, reminiscent of an uncleaned stable.

Characteristics Zebrano is available in large sizes, giving the
turner a lot of scope, and is usually sold as through-cut boards or
pre-dimensioned blanks. The heartwood is mainly straw to pale
buff-brown in colour, with random streaks of dark brown or
purplish-black. The sapwood is pale and rather featureless. The
combination of colours, resembling a zebra's stripe pattern, is very
attractive. The grain is usually interlocked and variable. The texture
is coarse and uneven, and the wood is hard, moderately heavy
and strong.

This is not the easiest of woods to turn. It cuts well with very
sharp gouges or skews, but scrapers make the surface woolly.
It sands well with the dry method, but watch out for heat-checks.
The wet method makes the surface murky because of colour
contamination from the dark streaks. It takes surface or
penetrative finishes well, but the grain may need filling.

Opepe
Nauclea diderrichii,
syn. *Sarcocephalus diderrichii*

Other names Akondoc, aloma, badi, bilinga,
kusia, kusiaba, linzi, n'gulu, maza

Grows Equatorial west Africa

Height 160ft (50m)

Trunk diameter 5ft (1.5m)

Specific gravity .74

Typical dry weight 46lb/ft³ (740kg/m³)

Possible health risks Dermatitis, irritation of
mucous membranes, dizziness, visual
disturbance, nosebleeds, blood spitting

Seasoning Opepe dries well if quartersawn, but when flatsawn
it is likely to check, split and distort. It is usually supplied in part-
seasoned boards or pre-dimensioned blanks, either through-cut or
square-edged, so the wood can be turned to completion as it is,
but will move and may split or check if not turned thin.
Alternatively it may be rough-turned, coated with PVA to
minimize checking or splitting, and set aside to season further.

Characteristics The heartwood is a uniform honey-yellow
when freshly cut, maturing on exposure to orange-brown or red-
brown with a distinctive coppery lustre. The sapwood looks quite
different, being a creamy grey-white and about 2in (50mm) thick.
The grain is usually interlocked or irregular, with a coarse to
medium texture. Ribbon or rope figures may give a striking
appearance to quartersawn surfaces. It can be used for joinery,
furniture and decorative turning.

The irregular and interlocking grain can prove tricky to work.
Very sharp gouges – or skews, for spindle work – used with a
slow, deliberate cut give the best finish off the tool and will result
in minimal grain tear-out. All other tools can and probably will lift
the grain and cause tear-out. It sands satisfactorily with either wet
or dry methods, but be careful of end-grain heat-checks, and do
not wet-sand if sapwood is present. It takes finishes readily and
can be brought to a high polish if needed. Some grain filling may
be required if you need an ultra-smooth finish.

Tasmanian myrtle
Nothofagus cunninghamii

Other names Tasmanian beech, myrtle beech, mountain beech, Australian nothofagus

Grows Tasmania and Victoria, Australia

Height 100–130ft (30–40m) or taller

Trunk diameter 3–5ft (0.9–1.5m)

Specific gravity .72

Typical dry weight 45lb/ft³ (720kg/m³)

Possible health risks Irritation to mucous membranes

Seasoning The outer, lighter wood dries easily, but the heartwood proper needs careful drying to avoid surface checking, internal honeycombing and collapse. The wood's movement can be used to good effect when wet-turning to completion. Kiln-dried wood is fine for joinery or furniture applications. Alternatively, rough-turn, leaving an extra ½–1in (13–25mm) or so of wall thickness per 12in (300mm) diameter to allow for movement, and coat with PVA to even out the drying process.

Characteristics This is a lovely wood to look at and to work with. The main heartwood, known as **red myrtle**, is pinkish-tan to sumptuous red-brown, with an outer zone of lighter colour between this and the narrow, pale cream sapwood. The grain is usually straight but may be slightly interlocked, and is sometimes slightly wavy, which results in some nice figure on quartersawn stock. The texture is fine, even and lustrous. It is not a true myrtle or beech. This dense hardwood has a moderate blunting effect on edge tools, and can be used for turning utilitarian or decorative items, and work related to joinery and cabinetmaking.

This wood cuts well whether wet, partially seasoned or fully seasoned. Bevel-rubbing tools give a slightly better cut than scrapers, but freshly honed scrapers should cause no more than minor blemishes on the end grain that can be removed very easily with abrasives. It sands and finishes well, but watch out for heat-checks on end grain.

Blackgum
Nyssa sylvatica

Other names Tupelo, black tupelo, tupelo gum, yellow gum tree, sour gum, wild pear tree, stinkwood

Grows USA, from Maine to Michigan, Illinois to Texas

Height 60–120ft (18–37m)

Trunk diameter 2–4ft (0.6–1.2m)

Specific gravity .46

Typical dry weight 29lb/ft³ (460kg/m³)

Possible health risks Not known

Seasoning Blackgum needs great care to prevent warping and twisting during drying. It can move a lot when drying, which makes it an excellent timber to experiment with wet turning, using a thin, even wall thickness. If stability is an issue, then rough-turn and set it aside to season.

Characteristics This is a lightweight wood, but very tough and capable of holding reasonably fine detail. It is hard-wearing enough to be used for flooring, furniture, joinery applications and decorative and functional turning. Its heartwood ranges from a pale creamy grey-brown or yellowish-tan to a soft brown. The sapwood is wide and lighter in colour, sometimes a creamy buff-brown. The grain is close and interlocked, the texture uniform. The overall appearance is very pleasant in a subtle way.

This wood is satisfactory to turn, but not one of the easiest. The interlocking grain can be a problem for skews and scrapers (less so for gouges), and can result in grain tear-out. Sharp tools traversed slowly across the work – using gouges or skew chisels in the case of spindle work – will be sufficient in most instances. Scrapers, used in conventional or shear-scraping mode, will not create as good a finish but can, with care, give a surface that requires only a small amount of sanding. The wood sands and finishes well, though oils darken the wood quite a lot. If you wish to maintain the creamy colour of the wood, use a surface finish such as lacquer containing UV inhibitors.

East African olive
Olea hochstetteri and *O. welwitschii*

Other names Olive, olivewood, ironwood, loliondo, musharagi, olmasi

Grows Cameroon, Congo, Ethiopia, Guinea, Ivory Coast, Kenya, Sierra Leone, Sudan, Tanzania, Uganda, Zambia

Height 24–30m (80–100ft)

Trunk diameter 0.6–0.9m (2–3ft)

Specific gravity .89

Typical dry weight 55lb/ft³ (890kg/m³)

Possible health risks Dust may irritate skin, eyes, nose and lungs

Seasoning The wood is slow to dry, with a tendency to check and split, and may honeycomb if dried too quickly. Kiln-drying is best. It is great for wet turning, but can also be turned partially seasoned if a bit of movement is acceptable. It can also be rough-turned and set aside to season further. It may be prudent to coat the rough-turned piece with PVA.

Characteristics A beautiful wood to look at and to work with. The heartwood is generally a buff-brown, with irregular darker streaks ranging from mid-brown to purplish-black, resulting in a marbled look. This is an oily wood, but not so much as European olive (*O. europaea*); the grain is usually straight, but sometimes interlocked, with a fine and even texture. The sapwood is creamy-yellow. The shavings can stain hands and steel, so make sure you clean up after turning. The wood is used for decorative and utilitarian turning, and for furniture and joinery components; it can also be carved.

This is a lovely wood to work, with only a minor risk of tear-out when one encounters interlocking grain; otherwise it works very well, producing a fine finish off the tool. It sands well, but beware of heat-checking. It may, however, prove resistant to some surface finishes, in which case you should wipe it over with a solvent such as cellulose thinners or methylated spirit (denatured alcohol) before applying the finish. There are no problems with penetrative finishes, and the surface can be taken to a high polish.

Desert ironwood
Olneya tesota

Other names Ironwood, Arizona ironwood, Sonora ironwood, palo de hierro, tesota

Grows Mexico, USA (Colorado, south-west Arizona, southern California)

Height 18–25ft (5.5–7.5m)

Trunk diameter 1ft 6in (0.46m)

Specific gravity .86

Typical dry weight 54lb/ft³ (860kg/m³)

Possible health risks Inhaled dust is unpleasant

Seasoning Very difficult: the wood is prone to cracks and checks which are often not visible on the surface. It can be turned from partially seasoned wood as long as the wall thickness is even. It seems to be stable and does not move or shrink much. Rough-turning also works.

Characteristics This is a beautiful wood. The heartwood can vary from a rich, honeyed golden-orange to dark reddish-brown, almost purplish-black, mottled with a golden orange-red. The narrow sapwood is a pale creamy-yellow. Sadly, the wood darkens quickly on exposure to light, becoming a more uniform deep brown colour. This is a brittle, extremely hard wood, with a high lustre. It appears to be available only in small sizes as sections of trunk or bough, which often contain splits or wormholes, or as pre-dimensioned blanks. Small decorative work is ideal for this wood. It carves well.

This is a tough wood that requires very sharp tools, traversed slowly across the wood, to achieve a good cut. On some pieces it is easier to achieve a good finish with scrapers than with bevel-rubbing tools. There is some dust produced when turning, and this has a strong, unpleasant, peppery smell that is difficult to describe. The wood can heat-check when sanding, so be careful. It can be sanded dry or wet, but only sand wet if no sapwood is present. It can be finished with both surface and penetrative finishes.

Lancewood

Oxandra lanceolata

Other names Yaya, asta, haya prieta, bois de lance

Grows Caribbean and Amazon

Height 50ft (15m)

Trunk diameter 1ft 6in (0.46m)

Specific gravity .81

Typical dry weight 51lb/ft³ (810kg/m³)

Possible health risks Not known

Seasoning This wood is fairly difficult to dry and has a high shrinkage rate. If the end grain is not sealed the wood will check badly. It can be turned to completion when wet or partially seasoned, in which case some movement will occur; or it can be rough-turned, coated with PVA and set aside to season further.

Characteristics The heartwood is dark silvery-brown. The creamy butter-yellow sapwood is the part that is typically encountered, unless you are able to obtain sections of the trunk or boughs where heartwood is present. The grain is usually straight and has a fine texture. It is only available in small sections, so the turner is restricted to small decorative work.

This is a hard but lovely wood to work with, though sadly it is quite bland to look at. It cuts well with all tools, sands easily and readily accepts finishes of all kinds. This sounds too good to be true, but if you have the opportunity to try this wood I think you will like it.

Avocado

Persea americana, syn. P. edulis, Laurus persea

Other names Persea, alligator pear, apricot (Virgin Islands); many other names in different countries

Grows Mexico, Guatemala, Honduras, USA (Hawaii, Florida and California)

Height 30–60ft (9–18m)

Trunk diameter 2ft 6in (0.76m)

Specific gravity .53

Typical dry weight 33lb/ft³ (530kg/m³)

Possible health risks Not known

Seasoning This wood can be kiln- or air-dried, but tends to warp during drying. It can be turned wet or partially seasoned to completion – in which case it will shrink and move – or rough-turned and set aside to season further.

Characteristics The heartwood is pink to light, creamy reddish-brown, while the wide sapwood is a milky off-white colour. The grain varies according to where the tree has grown, but is generally straight with a medium figuring. It has medium lustre and texture. The wood can be used for decorative or utilitarian work. It is only available in small to medium sizes, so possibilities are limited. It turns very well, carves well and is capable of holding quite fine detail.

Scrapers do not cut as cleanly as bevel-rubbing tools; even in shear-scraping mode they are likely to create a woolly surface or tear out the end grain a little. This is not a problem, since the finish that can be achieved with bevel-rubbing tools is so good that you can go straight to abrasives afterwards to remove any minor blemishes. Avocado sands and finishes well.

Celery-top pine

Phyllocladus rhomboidalis

Other names Not known

Grows Tasmania

Height 100ft (30m)

Trunk diameter 3ft (1m)

Specific gravity .64

Typical dry weight 40lb/ft³ (640kg/m³)

Possible health risks Not known

Seasoning This timber dries well with little degrade. If you are turning for joinery or cabinetmaking applications, you can get away with using kiln-dried sections. Partially seasoned wood can be turned, but will move, and if the walls are too thick they may check. If you require accuracy and stability you will need to season the wood further; one option is to rough-turn and set the piece aside to dry further.

Characteristics This softwood is not a true pine. The heartwood colour varies from a creamy pale yellow to a soft tan. The narrow sapwood is typically the same colour and not distinct from the heartwood. It has a straight grain with a fine, even texture. The growth rings are clearly defined and closely spaced. The wood carves well and can be used for both decorative and utilitarian work.

This is a lovely, clean wood to work with. It cuts well with skews and gouges, but does not respond well to scrapers no matter how they are used: scrapers will leave a woolly surface or tear out the grain, especially end grain. After using the bevel-rubbing tools, go straight to abrasives. It readily accepts either surface or penetrative finishes.

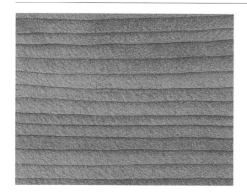

Sitka spruce

Picea sitchensis

Other names Silver spruce, tideland spruce, Menzies spruce, coast spruce, yellow spruce

Grows Western parts of North America, from northern Canada to Alaska

Height 125–200ft (38–60m)

Trunk diameter 3–6ft (0.9–1.8m)

Specific gravity .43

Typical dry weight 27lb/ft³ (430kg/m³)

Possible health risks Respiratory irritation, bronchial asthma, rhinitis and dermatitis

Seasoning This wood dries easily using both air-drying and kilning methods, though if larger sections are dried too fast there may be twisting and cupping. Young wood may have checks, splits and raised grain. Movement is medium to small. Trunk, boughs or part-seasoned sections can be turned green and allowed to distort. Turnings for joinery or cabinetmaking can use kiln-dried wood, but if you require even more stability, rough-turn the piece and set it aside to season further.

Characteristics Available in large sizes, this softwood has creamy-whitish to light pink-brown heartwood with a violet tinge, which darkens to a pink-tinged silver-brown. The sapwood is pale buttery-yellow and looks similar to the heartwood. The grain is usually straight, close and free of knots and defects, though wood from young trees may contain a significant proportion of spiral grain. The texture is fine, even and silky, especially in older-growth wood.

Being moderately soft and light yet strong, it is easy to work with sharp bevel-rubbing tools, which will leave a fine, silky surface. Scrapers tear the grain, so go from bevel-rubbing tools straight to abrasive. The wood has a slight resinous odour, and the resin can clog abrasives when sanding. It can be sanded dry or wet, and readily takes finishes of all descriptions. Softwoods are often overlooked by turners, except for architectural or joinery work. This is sad, because utilitarian ware and decorative work offer many worthwhile possibilities, and the results can look great.

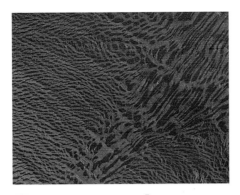

European plane

Platanus hybrida, syn. *P. acerifolia,*
P. x hispanica

Other names London plane, English plane, French plane. Related species include *P. orientalis* in South-east europe, Iran and Turkey; *P. occidentalis* (American plane), known as buttonwood or American sycamore.

Grows Europe

Height 100ft (30m)

Diameter of trunk 3–4ft (0.9–1.2m)

Specific gravity .62

Typical dry weight 39lb/ft³ (620kg/m³)

Possible health risks Not known

Seasoning Plane dries quickly, but care is needed to prevent splitting and distortion. It can, depending on the end use, be turned wet or partially seasoned to completion, or rough-turned and set aside to season.

Characteristics The heartwood is pinkish-tan or coppery-brown. On quartersawn stock the numerous, very conspicuous rays give a distinctive and attractive fleck figuring, known as **lacewood**. Plane has straight grain and a fine to medium texture. It can be used for decorative or utilitarian turning or for furniture parts, and carves reasonably well.

This wood cuts well with sharp tools. The end grain may tear out a little when scrapers are used conventionally, but shear-scraping minimizes this risk. Small pieces around the fleck figuring may also be liable to flake off; using sharp bevel-rubbing tools and then moving straight to abrasives is the best way of avoiding this. It sands well and can be finished easily with surface or penetrative finishes.

Bowl in plane
burr by Bert Marsh

Honey mesquite

Prosopis juliflora and *P. glandulosa*

Other names Honey locust, ironwood, Texas ironwood, algarroba, honeypod

Grows North and South America

Height 20–40ft (6–13m)

Trunk diameter up to 1ft 8in (0.5m)

Specific gravity .80

Typical dry weight 50lb/ft³ (800kg/m³)

Possible health risks Respiratory irritation, dermatitis

Seasoning Honey mesquite dries well, but small checks and splits can develop during air-drying. Partially seasoned or air-dried sections can be turned to completion, and rarely move much; but if you need to have absolute stability, then rough-turn the piece and set it aside to season. This is one of the most dimensionally stable woods you are ever likely to encounter – a real treat.

Characteristics This is a delightful wood to look at and to work with. The heartwood is a rich, deep honey-brown to dark copper-brown, with darker wavy lines. The texture is fine or medium, with straight or wavy open grain; occasionally the grain is irregular. It often exhibits beautiful figuring and produces stunning burrs (burls). The sapwood is up to 1in (25mm) thick and is pale creamy-white. This is a hard, tough, heavy wood, good for turning furniture and joinery parts as well as utilitarian and decorative wares. It can be carved with power tools.

Sharp tools are essential for a good finish. If the wood is old and very dry, a lot of dust can be produced, and end-grain tear-out is likely when using scrapers in conventional mode. Freshly seasoned wood is much more pleasant and easy to work, with tear-out likely only if the grain is irregular. Scrapers sometimes produce a finer surface than gouges or skews. Finishing can be a little tricky: I have found it resistant to some surface finishes. It does, however, readily accept oils, followed by waxes, and can be power-buffed to a fine polish. This wood is a delight – try some.

American cherry
Prunus serotina

Other names Black cherry, cabinet cherry, choke cherry, Edwards Plateau cherry, wild cherry, rum cherry, whisky cherry, New England mahogany

Grows Eastern and Midwestern USA, southern Canada

Height 80–100ft (24–30m)

Trunk diameter 2–5ft (0.6–1.5m)

Specific gravity .58

Typical dry weight 36lb/ft³ (580kg/m³)

Possible health risks Wheezing and dizziness

Seasoning It dries rapidly, but fast drying can cause severe distortion. Shrinkage is common and ring shakes can occur. It can be air-dried or kiln-dried, but the rate of drying must be controlled. If turning for joinery or cabinetmaking applications, working straight from kiln-dried stock is fine. Otherwise it can be turned wet or partially seasoned, or rough-turned and set aside to dry further.

Characteristics This wood looks nice and works well; I recommend trying it for both decorative and utilitarian work. It is available in quite large sizes, giving wide scope for experimenting. The heartwood is pale creamy-pink to light or mid coppery-brown, darkening on exposure to a rich, deep red-brown. It sometimes has attractive darker flecks and streaks running through it. The much paler sapwood is pink, tinged with cream. The grain is usually straight, the texture fine and even. It occasionally forms burrs (burls), which are highly sought-after.

It is an easy wood to work. Bevel-rubbing tools produce a very fine finish off the tool; scrapers less so, with a risk of tearing out the end grain if the tools are anything but sharp. It sands and finishes well.

Douglas fir
Pseudotsuga menziesii

Other names Blue Douglas fir, Oregon pine, British Columbian pine; also Colorado, Oregon, Rocky Mountain Douglas fir

Grows Canada and USA; also introduced to New Zealand, Australia and parts of Europe

Height 80–200ft (24–60m) or more

Trunk diameter 2–5ft (0.6–1.5m)

Specific gravity .53

Typical dry weight 33lb/ft³ (530kg/m³)

Possible health risks Dermatitis, nasal cancer, rhinitis, respiratory problems; splinters may become septic

Seasoning Drying is quick and easy, because of the low moisture content of the heartwood. Staining from extractives, ring failure and honeycombing occur occasionally. Partially seasoned timber is fine for many kinds of utilitarian or decorative work, but for joinery or furniture components kiln-drying is advisable. It rarely needs rough-turning, except for precision items such as boxes.

Characteristics The sapwood can be creamy-yellow or pinkish-white, and varies in thickness. The heartwood is variable in colour, and shows a very strong contrast between earlywood and latewood in the annual rings: summerwood is orange-brown or red-brown, while the softer springwood is a soft yellow-orange. The grain is normally straight but can be even or uneven, and is sometimes wavy or curly. Wood with narrow growth rings has a more uniform texture than that with wider rings, which are usually uneven. It is a great wood for furniture or joinery, but also very suitable for decorative and utilitarian turned wares.

Sharp bevel-rubbing tools are essential for a good finish. Scrapers, or tools which are less than sharp, will result in grain tear-out or a woolly surface, so avoid scrapers and go straight to abrasives. The wood sands well, but the abrasive is liable to clog and, because the wood is soft, sanding may create hollows if you do not keep the abrasive moving. It responds well to wet or dry sanding, and accepts oils and waxes well, but may require many coats of a surface finish to avoid patchiness.

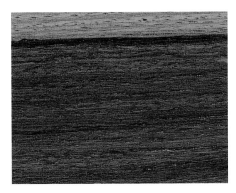

Muninga
Pterocarpus angolensis

Other names Mninga, bloodwood, brown African padauk, mukwa, kiaat, kajat, ambila

Grows Angola, Botswana, Namibia, Zimbabwe, Zambia, South Africa, Tanzania, Congo

Height 40–60ft (12–18m)

Trunk diameter 1ft 4in–2ft 6in (0.4–0.75m) or wider

Specific gravity .62

Typical dry weight 39lb/ft³ (620kg/m³)

Possible health risks Sawdust can cause dermatitis, nasal irritation and bronchial asthma

Seasoning The wood dries easily with almost no degrade, just like mesquite (*Prosopis glandulosa*). Lidded boxes require rough-turning, but most items can be turned from partially seasoned stock. Furniture and joinery parts and decorative turning are all suitable uses.

Characteristics This is a dense, heavy and hard wood. The greyish-yellow sapwood is clearly distinct from the heartwood, which ranges from a soft, honeyed golden-brown through a rich reddish-chocolate colour to a deep red or violet-brown with dark purple-brown or reddish irregular streaks. The grain can be straight or interlocking, with a medium texture. It sometimes exhibits mottled, striped or wavy figuring. Occasionally there are small white spots in the wood.

This attractive wood is satisfactory to work, but not one of the easiest. A fair amount of dust is produced. The edges are rather brittle and can break out. Tear-out is likely on the end grain and in areas of interlocking grain, if scrapers are used with anything but the most sensitive of cuts and a freshly honed edge. Bevel-rubbing tools give the best finish, but a slow, deliberate, delicate cut with a freshly sharpened tool is needed. The wood sands well, using dry or wet methods, but you should only wet-sand if there is no sapwood present. It readily accepts surface or penetrative finishes, and can be taken to a very high polish. The results are well worth the care that needs to be taken when working with this wood.

Andaman padauk
Pterocarpus dalbergioides

Other names Padauk, Andaman redwood, maidon, vermilion wood

Grows Andaman Islands

Height 80–120ft (25–37m)

Trunk diameter 3–5ft (0.9–1.5m)

Specific gravity .77

Typical dry weight 48lb/ft³ (770kg/m³)

Possible health risks Sawdust may cause itching, swollen eyelids, nasal irritation and vomiting

Seasoning It can be air- or kiln-dried with little danger of degrade, but may occasionally warp or split. It is available in large sizes, in boards or pre-dimensioned blanks. Projects can be turned to completion from wet or part-seasoned pieces, but will move a little; or they can be rough-turned and set aside to stabilize further.

Characteristics With its rich, luxuriant colours, this is to my mind the prima donna of all the padauks. It is also the slowest to lose its fresh-cut vibrancy. The heartwood ranges from a deep, honeyed orange-red to a darker, rich red-brown, with darker streaks of red, brown, violet or black. On exposure the wood becomes a deep, rich red-brown. The sapwood is narrow and clearly distinct from the heartwood, being off-white or yellow-grey. The wood has, in my experience, a waxy or oily feel, but not in the same way as olive (*Olea europaea*) or cocobolo (*Dalbergia retusa*). The irregular, interlocked or wavy grain produces a ribbon, roe or curly figure. It has a fairly coarse, uniform texture. This wood is typically used for furniture or decorative turning.

The interlocking, irregular grain can be a problem if you are using less than sharp tools, but slow, deliberate cuts with freshly sharpened edges should give good results. Bevel-rubbing tools produce the best surface. Scrapers have to be very sharp and used in a delicate manner to minimize grain tear-out. A lot of fine, sticky dust may be produced. It sands satisfactorily – though it will readily clog abrasives – and accepts finishes well.

Burma padauk

Pterocarpus macrocarpus

Other names Pradoo, mai pradoo, pterocarpus

Grows Myanmar (Burma), Laos, Philippines, Thailand, Vietnam

Height 80ft (24m)

Trunk diameter 2–3ft (0.6–0.9m) or more

Specific gravity .85

Typical dry weight 53lb/ft³ (850kg/m³)

Possible health risks Dermatitis, asthma, nasal irritation

Seasoning It dries with almost no degrade, apart from a risk of surface checking. Turning to completion from wet or part-seasoned wood is an option, as is rough-turning and setting it aside to season, depending on the project.

Characteristics Burma padauk is hard, heavy and dense. The heartwood ranges from a light, soft orange-red to deep, rich coppery-red, sometimes with dark lines when freshly cut. The wood changes colour considerably on exposure, becoming a rich, honeyed orange-brown. The narrow sapwood is a creamy off-white. The grain is usually interlocked, with a moderately coarse to medium texture. When quartersawn, it may display a ribbon-striped figure.

This wood should be worked in the same way as Andaman padauk (*P. dalbergioides*). However, Burma padauk can be a bit brittle and there is a risk of the edges fracturing or splintering off if a heavy-handed cut is made, so be careful and make slow, deliberate cuts. This wood also produces a fine, sticky dust during turning. It sands and finishes well.

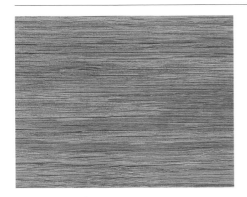

American white oak

Quercus alba, Q. prinus, Q. lobata, Q. michauxii, Q. lyrata

Other names Chestnut oak; swamp chestnut oak (*Q. michauxii*); overcup oak (*Q. lyrata*)

Grows Central North America and Canada

Height up to 100ft (30m)

Trunk diameter 0.9–1.2m (3–4ft)

Specific gravity .76

Typical dry weight 47lb/ft³ (760kg/m³)

Possible health risks Asthma, sneezing, nose and eye irritation, nasal cancer

Seasoning Can be kiln- or air-dried but has a tendency to split, check and honeycomb. It can be turned to completion from wet or from a partially seasoned state, but does warp. Kiln-dried wood is fine for joinery or furniture components. If more accuracy is required, it can be rough-turned and set aside to season further.

Characteristics This is a gem of a wood, and I find it easier to work than European oak (*Q. robur* or *Q. petraea*). The heartwood is creamy-brown to mid-tan, sometimes tinged with light red. The sapwood is a greyish off-white. The grain is straight and open with a medium-coarse texture, with large rays that give it a silver-grained appearance; the quartercut surface shows numerous rays and is very attractive. Various types of figuring can occur, including swirls, crotch figure and burrs. It can be used for many applications, including furniture and joinery components, utilitarian and artistic items.

The wood cuts cleanly in most circumstances with sharp gouges or skews. Scrapers can cause end-grain tear-out. If quartersawn stock is used, there is a marked increase in the risk of grain tear-out, especially when using scrapers. Other than that, it works well, leaving a nice finish off the tool, and sands and polishes well. If you require a very fine, smooth surface, grain filling may be required. As with all oaks, the shavings can stain iron, so make sure you clean the lathe and tools after turning.

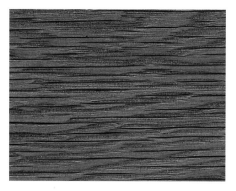

American red oak

Quercus rubra

Other names Red oak, northern red oak, Canadian red oak, grey oak; also sold with southern red oak or Spanish oak (*Q. falcata*) as 'red oak'

Grows Eastern Canada and USA; also Iran, Europe and UK

Height 60–90ft (18–27m)

Trunk diameter 3ft (1m)

Specific gravity .77

Typical dry weight 48lb/ft³ (770kg/m³)

Possible health risks Asthma, sneezing, eye and nose irritation, nasal cancer

Seasoning The wood dries slowly and is quite difficult to season. End-grain checking, ring failure, honeycombing and iron stains are distinctly possible. The project being tackled will dictate whether wet, partially or fully seasoned wood is required.

Characteristics The heartwood has a tan to mid reddish-brown colour. Red oak is not dissimilar to white oak, but is a little more pinkish-red in colour and has smaller rays, which results in a less pronounced figure. The grain is usually straight and open, but can vary. It generally has a coarse texture, but this also varies. The sapwood is off-white to light brown. This hard, heavy wood has a slight blunting effect on saws, but a bigger effect on turning tools, so frequent sharpening is necessary. It is available in large sizes, suitable for a wide range of projects.

It behaves and cuts in the same manner as *Q. alba*. Again, if a very smooth surface finish is required the grain will have to be filled before the application of a surface or penetrative finish.

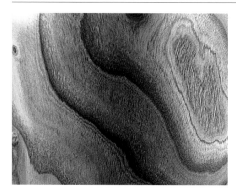

Staghorn sumac

Rhus typhina

Other names Sumac, hairy sumac, velvet sumac, American sumac, vinegar tree; the name may also be spelt **sumach**

Grows USA, UK and parts of mainland Europe

Height up to 40ft (12m)

Trunk diameter 1ft (0.3m)

Specific gravity .45

Typical dry weight 34lb/ft³ (545kg/m³)

Possible health risks Not known

Seasoning It is easy to air-dry, and not prone to cracks or other defects. Once dried, the sticky exudation from between bark and wood ceases. The wood is not sold commercially, but the tree is grown in gardens and sections can sometimes be had from tree surgeons. Pieces can be wet-turned to completion, or rough-turned and set aside to season. If left in the round, there is a risk of end-splitting, so sealing the ends after dimensioning is a must.

Characteristics This lovely wood shows a dramatic contrast between sap and heart. It has the greenest colour of any timber I know. The heartwood is a greenish orange-brown or honey-yellow; the sapwood is narrow and creamy-white. The wood is light, soft and brittle, with visible growth rings and ring pores. Sadly, it fades to a deeper brown, but it retains the green tinge.

The wood cuts best when wet or partially seasoned; I use sharp bevel-rubbing tools followed by abrasive. Dry wood can be dusty, and is prone to grain tear-out, especially with scrapers. The central pith is soft, but it is hard to avoid using it since the wood only comes in small sizes. I put a few drops of cyanoacrylate adhesive on it; once this is hard, the pith can safely be turned. Be careful when sanding to keep the abrasive moving: if you dwell in one place, hollows will form. The wood shows every scratch, so sand carefully and do not skip grades. It will heat-check if too much heat is generated. It readily takes surface and penetrative finishes, and can be brought to a high polish.

Willow

Salix spp.

Other names Black willow, swamp willow, Gooding willow, Dudley willow (*S. nigra*); white or common willow (*S. alba*); cricket-bat willow (*S. alba* var. *coerulea*); crack willow (*S. fragilis*)

Grows Europe, western and central Asia, North Africa, North America

Height 70–90ft (21–27m)

Trunk diameter 3–4ft (0.9–1.2m)

Specific gravity .45

Typical dry weight 28lb/ft³ (450kg/m³)

Possible health risks Sensitizer. Those who are allergic to aspirin may be allergic to willow

Seasoning This wood may warp during seasoning if care is not taken. Crack willow (*S. fragilis*) can split badly when drying. All species are liable to retain pockets of moisture. The wood can be turned to completion when wet or partially seasoned; expect a fair amount of movement, which can be exploited to good effect. Seasoned wood, especially when kiln-dried, can be turned to completion with only a little movement – unless it is highly figured, in which case I have known a lot of distortion to occur. For accurate work I favour rough-turning and setting aside to season, leaving extra wall thickness to allow for the likely movement.

Characteristics This is a quite a lightweight timber. Willow in general has a creamy-white sapwood with a creamy, pink-tinged heartwood. Black willow's heartwood varies from reddish-tan to silvery-brown, and the sapwood is creamy-red or light fawn. The grain is usually straight, but can be interlocked, and the wood has a uniform texture. It can at times exhibit a wonderful mottled figuring. It is suitable for carving.

Willow cuts best with very sharp gouges and skews, used with a delicate, slow cut; even so, a woolly surface may result, especially on wet wood. After shaping with these tools, go straight to abrasives to remove minor blemishes. Scrapers will create a woolly surface that requires a lot of abrasive work to get clean. The wood sands and finishes well. It takes on a pleasant warm patina if finished with oil.

American sassafras

Sassafras officinale and *S. albidum*

Other names Red sassafras, saxifrax tree, golden elm, cinnamon wood, black ash, aguetree

Grows Eastern USA

Height 40–90ft (12–27m)

Trunk diameter 2–5ft (0.6–1.5m)

Specific gravity .45

Typical dry weight 28lb/ft³ (450kg/m³)

Possible health risks Skin and respiratory irritation; possibly carcinogenic

Seasoning It requires care in drying as it tends to check slightly, but it can be kiln- or air-dried. It can be turned to completion from wet or partially seasoned stock if movement is acceptable, or rough-turned and set aside to season further for precision items such as boxes. Kilned stock is fine for joinery or furniture parts.

Characteristics This is a very pleasant, aromatic timber. The heartwood is light brown when freshly cut, darkening to a matt, coppery red-brown. The narrow sapwood is yellowish-white. The wood has a coarse texture and the grain is generally straight, but it can be a bit brittle. It is quite a soft timber. The grain figuring is often compared to that of white ash (*Fraxinus americana*), and it has quite a pleasant smell. It can be used for cabinetmaking, joinery, decorative and utilitarian turning.

This is a pleasant wood to turn. It is, however, another of those woods for which I would recommend using bevel-rubbing tools first, then skipping scrapers – which will tear the grain – and going straight to abrasives to remove any blemishes. Do keep the abrasive moving, to avoid creating unwanted hollows. The wood sands and finishes well. I like using an oil finish, which imparts a nice silky feel and a warm glow to the wood after a few coats. That said, it also finishes well with lacquers and other surface finishes.

Bowl by
Bert Marsh

Lilac

Syringa vulgaris

Other names Not known

Grows Europe, Asia, northern USA

Height 10–15ft (3–4.5m) on average

Trunk diameter 3–6in (75–150mm)

Specific gravity .72

Typical dry weight 45lb/ft³ (720kg/m³)

Possible health risks Not known

Seasoning This wood is difficult to season without checking: if left in the log or as branches it will split badly. The best way to dry lilac is to cut it along the centre of the log, seal the ends with sealant or PVA and leave it to season. Alternatively the wood can be turned wet, using a thin, even wall thickness; or rough-turned and set aside to season, again using PVA to retard moisture loss. Even when PVA is used there will be quite a high failure rate, so I prefer to turn wet or part-seasoned wood to completion.

Characteristics A member of the olive family (Oleaceae), lilac is really a large shrub, but it grows to the size of a small tree. It is not sold commercially, but is more likely to be obtained from someone who is removing it from the garden. The very narrow sapwood is pale cream with visible growth rings. This wood is very pleasant to look at and to work. The heartwood is a creamy, buttery colour with pinkish-violet streaks, but varies a lot; it has a fine, uniform grain and texture. The central pith or core of the tree can be soft; you may need to avoid it altogether, or you could stabilize it with cyanoacrylate adhesive. Lilac carves well.

It is easy to work with bevel-rubbing tools. Shear-scraping gives a better finish than conventional scraping. It sands satisfactorily, but watch out for heat-checking. It accepts finishes readily. The wood has a sweet, pleasant smell reminiscent of the tree's fragrant flowers. Oils are my favourite finishes for this wood, but lacquers work well also. Sadly, the sizes available limit its use to small items.

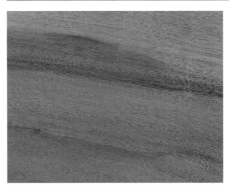

Primavera

Tabebuia donnell-smithii

Other names Duranga, San Juan, palo blanco, cortez, cortez blanco, roble

Grows Central America

Height 75–100ft (23–30m)

Trunk diameter 2–3ft (0.6–0.9m) or more

Specific gravity .45

Typical dry weight 28lb/ft³ (450kg/m³)

Possible health risks Not known

Seasoning Primavera dries easily with little degrade, but there may be some warping and checking. For joinery or furniture parts, it can be turned to completion from kiln-dried wood. It can be worked from wet or partially seasoned stock, but expect a small amount of movement. It responds well to rough-turning and setting aside to season before finish-turning.

Characteristics This pleasant-looking timber is used a lot in joinery and cabinetmaking, but it is also a delightful wood for decorative turning. It can be carved as well. It starts off a soft buttery-cream colour, darkening on exposure to a reddish honey colour with streaks of pink, orange, red and various shades of brown. It can have straight, interlocked or wavy grain, and may have a good ribbon, mottle, roey or narrow fiddleback figure. The wood has a medium to coarse texture.

It is a light wood that cuts well with gouges and skews, but not so well with scrapers, which can tear out the grain, especially when it is interlocking or wavy. The wood is quite soft, so be careful when sanding and keep the abrasive moving so as not to create hollows. It is easy to sand and finish, though grain filling may be needed if you require a very smooth surface.

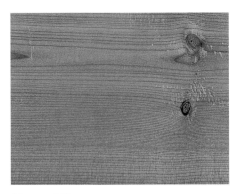

Pacific yew

Taxus brevifolia

Other names Yew, western yew

Grows Western North America from southern Alaska to California

Height 20–40ft (6–12m)

Trunk diameter 12–15in (0.3–0.4m)

Specific gravity .62

Typical dry weight 39lb/ft³ (620kg/m³)

Possible health risks Precautions should be taken to avoid inhaling dust, which has been shown to cause swelling and skin or nasal sensitivity in some people

Seasoning Slow drying is essential to reduce the risk of serious shakes. End grain should be sealed; this applies to boards as well as rough-turned pieces. The wood responds well to turning from either a wet or a part-seasoned state; it can also be rough-turned. The bark is thin and can be incorporated into the design.

Characteristics The heartwood goes from a light orange to orange-brown or red-brown, and is clearly distinct from the narrow, creamy off-white sapwood. It has a close, fine grain and a fine, even texture, and is capable of holding fine detail. This wood can form wonderful burrs (burls) which vary in figure from small clusters of pips to areas of swirling grain, showing a variety of colours from orange-tan to reds, purples and browns. It can be used for furniture and joinery components as well as decorative or utilitarian wares. However, like European yew (*T. baccata*), it may be inadvisable for items in contact with food.

It is easier and pleasanter to work than European yew: it usually has straighter grain and is less prone to end-grain tear-out. A good finish is achieved with bevel-rubbing tools, but scrapers give variable results. Old wood produces a fair amount of harmful dust. It can heat-check when sanding, so be careful; otherwise it sands well as long as you don't skip grades. It takes finishes readily, although penetrative finishes such as oils can darken the wood considerably. If you want to maintain the delicate orange colour, use a surface finish such as lacquer or melamine.

Teak

Tectona grandis

Other names Burma teak

Grows India, Myanmar (Burma), Thailand, Vietnam; plantations in other tropical countries

Height up to 150ft (45m)

Trunk diameter 6–8ft (1.8–2.4m)

Specific gravity .65

Typical dry weight 40lb/ft³ (650kg/m³)

Possible health risks Dermatitis, conjunctivitis, irritation to nose and throat, swelling of the scrotum, nausea, over-sensitivity to light

Seasoning Teak kiln-dries and air-dries well. Furniture or joinery parts can be made from kiln-dried stock. Part-seasoned material can be used, but items that need to maintain their shape are best rough-turned and set aside to season.

Characteristics The heartwood is honey-brown or reddish-brown, sometimes with dark markings, and darkens considerably on exposure. The sapwood is a pale, creamy yellow-brown, and can be narrow or of medium width. The grain is usually straight but sometimes wavy or interlocking, giving an attractive figure. The texture is rather coarse and uneven, and it has an oily or waxy feel. Straight-grained wood carves well. Silica deposits, visible as white or grey flecks, can have a severe blunting effect on tools.

Teak will cut well and produce a fine surface on one project, and on another it will rip the edges off tools as though you were rubbing them on cement. Wavy or irregular grain can tear out easily. That said, in the main it is relatively easy to work. Scrapers will not produce as clean a surface as gouges or skews, but with sharp tools and a delicate cut a good finish is possible. Lots of fine, oily, noxious dust is produced, more so when working with very dry or old wood. It heat-checks on end grain if too much heat is produced, and readily clogs abrasives. The wood's oily nature means that some surface finishes do not bond well; wiping over with solvent should help. Teak readily accepts penetrative finishes. The end result is well worth the effort.

Indian laurel

*Terminalia alata, T. coriacea, T. crenulata,
T. elliptica syn. T. tomentosa*

Other names Taukkyan, asna, cay, hanta,
neang, mutti, sain

Grows India, Myanmar (Burma), Bangladesh
and Pakistan

Height 100ft (30m)

Trunk diameter 3ft (1m)

Specific gravity .86

Typical dry weight 53lb/ft³ (860kg/m³)

Possible health risks Dust can be an irritant

Seasoning It is liable to surface checks, splits and warping. Slow drying reduces degrade. It can be turned to completion partially seasoned, but will move. It may be worked kiln-dry for joinery or cabinetmaking purposes, but rough-turning is also an option.

Characteristics The pinkish sapwood is clearly differentiated from the heartwood, which varies from reddish light or mid-brown with fine dark streaks, to a dark burnt umber with darker bands or streaks. The grain is usually fairly straight, but often interlocked or irregular. The texture is coarse to medium. Quartersawn timber can have an attractive figure. It is harder and denser than teak (*Tectona grandis*), and not as pleasant to work. It produces a dirty dust which may contain minute splinters. It is brittle and prone to chipping at the edges; it blunts tools severely, and interlocking grain is very likely to tear out. Partially seasoned wood cuts a little more easily, with less dust, than kiln-dried wood; however, it will move more than kiln-dried wood once turned – not much more, but too much for boxes or platters.

Many books claim that it is easy to turn, but that is not my experience. The best cuts are made with sharp bevel-rubbing tools, but it does scrape satisfactorily if a very light touch is made with a freshly honed scraper. I find conventional scraping better than shear-scraping. It cuts well with abrasives, but will clog them quite quickly. It finishes well. Oils add some extra warmth to the colour – otherwise this wood can look a little stark.

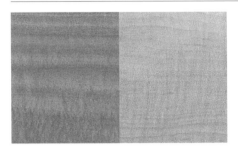

T. vulgaris   *T. americana*

Lime and basswood

Tilia vulgaris and T. americana

Other names Linden (*T. vulgaris*); American lime, American whitewood, American linden (*T. americana*)

Grows Europe, including UK (*T. vulgaris*); eastern Canada and USA (*T. americana*)

Height 80–100ft (25–30m)

Trunk diameter up to 4ft (1.2m)

Specific gravity .54 (*T. vulgaris*); .41 (*T. americana*)

Typical dry weight 34lb/ft³ (540kg/m³) (*T. vulgaris*); 26lb/ft³ (410kg/m³) (*T. americana*)

Possible health risks Not known

Seasoning The wood dries at a rapid rate and can distort. Slow kilning minimizes degrade, but it can also be turned to completion wet or from partially seasoned stock; conversely it can be rough-turned and set aside to season further.

Characteristics European lime is denser than basswood, and holds finer detail; but for turning purposes there is little to choose between them and they may be considered together. Lime is probably better known as a carving timber, for which it is superb, but it is great for turning joinery and furniture parts, or for decorative or utilitarian work. It holds fine detail and, though plain to look at, its subtle colour and figure are very effective when a clean, fresh look is required so as not to overwhelm the form. The wood is initially a soft, creamy pale yellow or uniform off-white to pinkish-tan, but ages eventually to a uniform light golden-brown. The grain is usually straight but sometimes irregular, with a fine and uniform texture; generally there is little or no figure, but it can display a ripple or mottled figure at times. Lime can also form burrs (burls); those I have encountered were of a tight, pippy cluster formation. The sapwood looks similar to the heartwood.

This wood cuts well with sharp skews and gouges; less so with scrapers, which can create a woolly surface unless you slow down the rate of traverse and make a shear cut. Lime sands well, but be careful not to sand hollows in the work or destroy fine detail. It readily accepts finishes and stains.

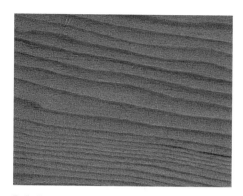

Western hemlock
Tsuga heterophylla

Other names Pacific hemlock, British Columbian hemlock, west coast hemlock, hemlock spruce, Alaska pine

Grows Western Canada and USA, UK, China and Japan

Height 100–150ft (30–46m)

Trunk diameter 3–4ft (0.9–1.2m)

Specific gravity .50

Typical dry weight 31lb/ft³ (500kg/m³)

Possible health risks Bronchial problems, rhinitis, dermatitis, eczema, possibly nasal cancer

Seasoning It dries slowly but well. Possible problems include shakes, uneven moisture content, iron stains and warping; when kiln-dried, there may be fine surface checks. Kiln-dried timber is fine for most of the projects this wood is used for: furniture and joinery parts, or utilitarian work.

Characteristics Hemlock is a softwood. The sapwood is around 3–5in (75–125mm) thick and looks similar to the heartwood, which is creamy-tan to pale golden-brown. Latewood areas are darker and exhibit hues of pinkish-orange, violet or rose-tan. A growth-ring figure is likely to be present on plainsawn surfaces. There may also be dark streaks caused by maggots, known as 'bird pecks'. The grain is normally straight and even, with a medium to fine texture. I really enjoy the bold growth-ring figuring.

The wood cuts cleanly with very sharp gouges and skews. Do not be tempted to use scrapers unless you are willing to accept a torn surface, or are prepared to spend a lot of time sanding. Instead, after turning with bevel-rubbing tools, go straight to abrasives to remove minor blemishes. Hemlock sands and finishes well.

American elm
Ulmus americana

Other names Elm, American white elm, Florida elm, soft elm, water elm. There are six species of elm in North America with similar characteristics

Grows Canada and USA

Height 100ft (30m)

Trunk diameter 2–4ft (0.6–1.2m)

Specific gravity .56

Typical dry weight 35lb/ft³ (560kg/m³)

Possible health risks Dermatitis; dust is an irritant to nose and eyes

Seasoning It may warp or twist during seasoning, sometimes severely if dried too quickly; ring failure can also occur, but splitting is unlikely. If drying in a kiln, keep temperatures low. Depending on the project, it can be turned to completion using wet, part-seasoned or kiln-dried wood. Rough-turning and setting it aside to dry is recommended for projects where accuracy is needed.

Characteristics This is a pleasant wood to look at and to work. It is not as showy in colour or figuring as English or wych elm (*U. procera*, *U. glabra*), but has a more subtle, mellow appearance which I find attractive. The heartwood is light silver-brown, tan or mid-brown, with hints of red. The wide sapwood is a light silvery-brown or reddish-brown. The grain can be straight or irregular and occasionally exhibits figuring. The texture is coarse. The wood is great for joinery and furniture, as well as utilitarian and decorative turned items.

Its working qualities are much the same as for English elm, though it is a little softer and scrapers can leave a woolly surface. It can be a little tricky with some surface finishes, requiring multiple coats to ensure an even appearance. Oil, however, seems to work fine.

Wych elm

Ulmus glabra

Other names Elm, mountain elm, white elm, Scots elm, Scotch elm, Irish leamhan

Grows UK (north and west), Ireland, Europe, western Asia

Height 130ft (40m)

Trunk diameter 5ft (1.5m)

Specific gravity .67

Typical dry weight 42lb/ft³ (670kg/m³)

Possible health risks Dermatitis, nasal cancer; dust can be an irritant

Seasoning This wood dries fairly rapidly and successfully, but can distort unless it is dried with closely spaced stickering. It can be turned to completion using wet or part-seasoned stock. Kiln-dried stock will be fine for most joinery and cabinetmaking situations, but rough-turning and setting it aside to season further is essential when very stable timber is required.

Characteristics This is a very pretty species of elm. The heartwood is light to mid-umber, with a greenish tinge or green streaking. The amount of green varies considerably, as does the colour: I have had pieces with none, but others have had many streaks in various shades of green. The sapwood is pale and distinct from the heartwood when freshly cut. The grain is usually straight, with a medium texture. It is usually finer and straighter than English elm (*U. procera*). The tree sometimes forms burrs, and the wood can also exhibit an attractive figure if the grain is crossed or interlocking. Uses include turning for joinery and furniture, utilitarian and artistic items.

The wood responds to turning in the same way as English elm.

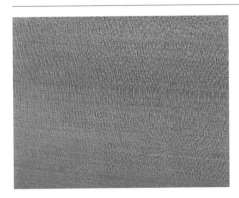

West Indian satinwood

Zanthoxylum flavum, syn. F. flava

Other names Jamaican satinwood, aceitillo, espinillo, yellow sanders, yellow wood, yellowheart

Grows Caribbean and southern Florida, USA

Height 40ft (12m)

Trunk diameter 1ft 3in–1ft 8in (0.4–0.5m)

Specific gravity .73

Typical dry weight 45lb/ft³ (730kg/m³)

Possible health risks Dermatitis

Seasoning This is a slow-drying wood. I have only been able to obtain air-dried sections, which moved a little when turned – not much, but enough to be noticeable on bowls, platters and boxes. No movement occurred on items that were rough-turned and allowed to season, but some developed surface checks. Coating rough-turned pieces with PVA greatly reduces surface checking.

Characteristics This is an excellent wood for decorative items, but is also used in furniture. The sapwood darkens from the bark until it merges with the heartwood, which is a light buttery colour at first, darkening to a pale orange or honeyed tan colour. The grain is typically interlocked or irregular, with a fine, even texture and a high lustre. There may be a roey or mottle figure.

This dense, heavy wood has a moderate blunting effect on edge tools. It can hold fine detail, but parts of it may be brittle and liable to break out, so care is needed; this applies to the edges of work as well as any fine detail such as beads, fillets and coves. It cuts well with sharp tools and a slow, deliberate cut. Scrapers can cause grain tear-out in places, but light cuts with freshly honed tools work in most circumstances. The wood is prone to heat-checking if too much heat is generated, but apart from that it sands well. A fine dust is produced which has quite a pleasant smell; I found that the smell lingered for a while even though extraction was used. It readily accepts both surface and penetrative finishes, and can be taken to a high polish if required.

Tulip tree (*Liriodendron tulipifera*), the source of American tulipwood

Further reading

The Australian Timber Buyer's Guide (Rozelle, NSW: Skills Publishing, 1994) ISBN 0 646 18096 7

Bishop, Peter, *100 Woods: A Guide to Popular Timbers of the World* (Marlborough, Wilts.: Crowood Press, 1999) ISBN 1 86126 167 5

Chapman, Robert, *Woodturning: A Fresh Approach* (Lewes, East Sussex: GMC Publications, 1999) ISBN 1 86108 119 7

Dresdner, Michael M., *The New Wood Finishing Book* (Newtown, CT: Taunton, 1999) ISBN 1 56158 299 9

Flynn, James H., Jr, and Holder, Charles D. (eds.), *A Guide to Useful Woods of the World*, 2nd edn. (Madison, WI: Forest Products Society, 2001) ISBN 1 892529 15 7

Hoadley, R. Bruce, *Identifying Wood: Accurate Results with Simple Tools* (Newtown, CT: Taunton, 1990) ISBN 0 942391 04 7

—, *Understanding Wood: A Craftsman's Guide to Wood Technology* (Newtown, CT: Taunton, 2000) ISBN 1 56158 358 8

Jackson, Albert, and Day, David, *Collins Good Wood Guide* (London: HarperCollins, 1996) ISBN 0 00 412997 0

O'Donnell, Michael, *Turning Green Wood* (Lewes, East Sussex: GMC Publications, 2000) ISBN 1 86108 089 1

Peters, Rick, *Woodworker's Guide to Wood: Softwoods, Hardwoods, Plywoods, Composites, Veneers* (New York: Sterling, 2000) ISBN 0 8069 3687 8

Porter, Terry, *Wood: Identification & Use* (Lewes, East Sussex: GMC Publications, 2004) ISBN 1 86108 377 7

Raffan, Richard, *Turned-Bowl Design* (Newtown, CT: Taunton, 1987) ISBN 0 918804 82 5

Wood and How to Dry it: The Best of Fine Woodworking Magazine (Newtown, CT: Taunton, 1986) ISBN 0 918804 54 X

Remember also that the Internet can be a great source of information regarding timbers, drying and seasoning, finishing and so on.

Publisher contact details

The Crowood Press Ltd
The Stable Block, Crowood Lane, Ramsbury, Marlborough, Wiltshire SN8 2HR, England
Tel: 01672 520320
Website: www.crowoodpress.co.uk

Forest Products Society
2801 Marshall Ct., Madison, WI 53705-2295, USA
Tel.: 608 231 1361
Website: www.forestprod.org

Guild of Master Craftsman Publications Ltd
Castle Place, 166 High Street, Lewes, East Sussex, BN7 1XU, England
Tel.: 01273 477374
Website: www.gmcbooks.com

HarperCollins Publishers
10 East 53rd Street, New York, NY 10022, USA
Tel.: 212 207 7000
Website: www.harpercollins.com

Skills Publishing Pty Ltd
8 Livingstone Street, Lawson, NSW 2783, Australia
Tel.: (02) 4759 2844
Website: www.skillspublish.com.au

Sterling Publishing Co., Inc.
387 Park Avenue South, New York, NY 10016, USA
Tel.: 212 532 7160
Website: www.sterlingpub.com

The Taunton Press, Inc.
63 South Main St., PO Box 5506, Newtown, CT 06470-5506, USA
Tel.: 203 426 8171
Website: www.taunton.com

About the author

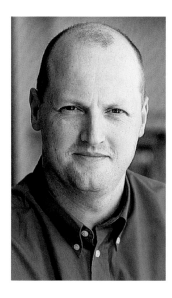

Mark Baker has always been fascinated by wood. The ability to work with such a wonderful medium, and to create something that will be admired, is fantastic, despite the occasional frustrations.

His father and a couple of uncles were carpenters and joiners, and, on leaving school, Mark in turn served a five-year apprenticeship in carpentry and joinery with a local building firm, where his duties included restoration work. He then helped to set up an industrial workshop for autistic adults. He obtained qualifications in teaching adults with special needs, and attained the level of Senior Instructor. Following this, he went to work as product manager for one of the major manufacturers of woodturning tools in Sheffield. From here, he was headhunted to be the editor of GMC's *Woodturning* magazine, and in addition he is now Group Editor of GMC's whole range of woodworking magazines.

He has demonstrated in the USA, Canada and Europe, and loves meeting turners from around the world.

Mark's first book, *Woodturning Projects: A Workshop Guide to Shapes*, is also published by GMC.

Index of common names

Index of botanical names

Titles available from
GMC Publications
Books

Woodcarving

Beginning Woodcarving	GMC Publications
Carving Architectural Detail in Wood: The Classical Tradition	
	Frederick Wilbur
Carving Birds & Beasts	GMC Publications
Carving Classical Styles in Wood	Frederick Wilbur
Carving the Human Figure: Studies in Wood and Stone	Dick Onians
Carving Nature: Wildlife Studies in Wood	Frank Fox-Wilson
Celtic Carved Lovespoons: 30 Patterns	Sharon Littley & Clive Griffin
Decorative Woodcarving (New Edition)	Jeremy Williams
Elements of Woodcarving	Chris Pye
Figure Carving in Wood: Human and Animal Forms	Sara Wilkinson
Lettercarving in Wood: A Practical Course	Chris Pye
Relief Carving in Wood: A Practical Introduction	Chris Pye
Woodcarving for Beginners	GMC Publications
Woodcarving Made Easy	Cynthia Rogers
Woodcarving Tools, Materials & Equipment (New Edition in 2 vols.)	
	Chris Pye

Woodturning

Bowl Turning Techniques Masterclass	Tony Boase
Chris Child's Projects for Woodturners	Chris Child
Decorating Turned Wood: The Maker's Eye	Liz & Michael O'Donnell
Green Woodwork	Mike Abbott
A Guide to Work-Holding on the Lathe	Fred Holder
Keith Rowley's Woodturning Projects	Keith Rowley
Making Screw Threads in Wood	Fred Holder
Segmented Turning: A Complete Guide	Ron Hampton
Turned Boxes: 50 Designs	Chris Stott
Turning Green Wood	Michael O'Donnell
Turning Pens and Pencils	Kip Christensen & Rex Burningham
Wood for Woodturners	Mark Baker
Woodturning: Forms and Materials	John Hunnex
Woodturning: A Foundation Course (New Edition)	Keith Rowley
Woodturning: A Fresh Approach	Robert Chapman
Woodturning: An Individual Approach	Dave Regester
Woodturning: A Source Book of Shapes	John Hunnex
Woodturning Masterclass	Tony Boase
Woodturning Projects: A Workshop Guide to Shapes	Mark Baker

Woodworking

Beginning Picture Marquetry	Lawrence Threadgold
Carcass Furniture	GMC Publications
Celtic Carved Lovespoons: 30 Patterns	Sharon Littley & Clive Griffin
Celtic Woodcraft	Glenda Bennett
Celtic Woodworking Projects	Glenda Bennett
Complete Woodfinishing (Revised Edition)	Ian Hosker
David Charlesworth's Furniture-Making Techniques	
	David Charlesworth
David Charlesworth's Furniture-Making Techniques – Volume 2	
	David Charlesworth

Furniture Projects with the Router	Kevin Ley
Furniture Restoration (Practical Crafts)	Kevin Jan Bonner
Furniture Restoration: A Professional at Work	John Lloyd
Furniture Workshop	Kevin Ley
Green Woodwork	Mike Abbott
History of Furniture: Ancient to 1900	Michael Huntley
Intarsia: 30 Patterns for the Scrollsaw	John Everett
Making Heirloom Boxes	Peter Lloyd
Making Screw Threads in Wood	Fred Holder
Making Woodwork Aids and Devices	Robert Wearing
Mastering the Router	Ron Fox
Pine Furniture Projects for the Home	Dave Mackenzie
Router Magic: Jigs, Fixtures and Tricks to	
Unleash your Router's Full Potential	Bill Hylton
Router Projects for the Home	GMC Publications
Router Tips & Techniques	Robert Wearing
Routing: A Workshop Handbook	Anthony Bailey
Routing for Beginners (Revised and Expanded Edition)	Anthony Bailey
Stickmaking: A Complete Course	Andrew Jones & Clive George
Stickmaking Handbook	Andrew Jones & Clive George
Storage Projects for the Router	GMC Publications
Success with Sharpening	Ralph Laughton
Veneering: A Complete Course	Ian Hosker
Veneering Handbook	Ian Hosker
Wood: Identification & Use	Terry Porter
Woodworking Techniques and Projects	Anthony Bailey
Woodworking with the Router: Professional	
Router Techniques any Woodworker can Use	Bill Hylton & Fred Matlack

Upholstery

Upholstery: A Beginners' Guide	David James
Upholstery: A Complete Course (Revised Edition)	David James
Upholstery Restoration	David James
Upholstery Techniques & Projects	David James
Upholstery Tips and Hints	David James

Dolls' Houses and Miniatures

1/12 Scale Character Figures for the Dolls' House	James Carrington
Americana in 1/12 Scale: 50 Authentic Projects	
	Joanne Ogreenc & Mary Lou Santovec
The Authentic Georgian Dolls' House	Brian Long
A Beginners' Guide to the Dolls' House Hobby	Jean Nisbet
Celtic, Medieval and Tudor Wall Hangings in 1/12 Scale Needlepoint	
	Sandra Whitehead
Creating Decorative Fabrics: Projects in 1/12 Scale	Janet Storey
Dolls' House Accessories, Fixtures and Fittings	Andrea Barham
Dolls' House Furniture: Easy-to-Make Projects in 1/12 Scale	Freida Gray
Dolls' House Makeovers	Jean Nisbet
Dolls' House Window Treatments	Eve Harwood
Edwardian-Style Hand-Knitted Fashion for 1/12 Scale Dolls	
	Yvonne Wakefield

Photography

Art Techniques

Videos

Magazines

Woodturning ◆ Woodcarving ◆ Furniture & Cabinetmaking
The Router ◆ New Woodworking ◆ The Dolls' House Magazine
Outdoor Photography ◆ Black & White Photography
Knitting ◆ Guild News

The above represents a full list of all titles currently published or scheduled to be published.
All are available direct from the Publishers or through bookshops, newsagents and specialist retailers.
To place an order, or to obtain a complete catalogue, contact:

GMC Publications,
Castle Place, 166 High Street, Lewes, East Sussex BN7 1XU United Kingdom
Tel: 01273 488005 Fax: 01273 402866
E-mail: pubs@thegmcgroup.com
Website: www.gmcbooks.com
Orders by credit card are accepted